UNIVERSE

UNIVERSE

TIME, SPACE, LIFE, GOD

~ HOW THINGS FIT TOGETHER ~

NIGEL T. FAITHFULL

Copyright © 2017, Nigel T. Faithfull

All rights reserved. No part of this book may be reproduced, scanned, or distributed in any printed or electronic form without permission.

Unless otherwise noted, Scripture quotations are taken from The Holy Bible, English Standard Version® (ESV®) Copyright © 2001 by Crossway, a publishing ministry of Good News Publishers. All rights reserved. ESV Text Edition: 2016

First Edition: 2017

ISBN: 978-0-9996559-0-0

20171211/LSI

Great Writing Publications
www.greatwriting.org
Taylors, SC, USA

Dedication

This book is dedicated to all who are searching for meaning and purpose, and how their lives fit into the awesome puzzle of God's universe.

Contents

Appreciations 9

Acknowledgements 11

Foreword: Dr. Geoff Thomas 12

Introduction 16

Chapter 1: Time 19

Chapter 2: Space 87

Chapter 3: Life 119

Chapter 4: God 173

Bibliography for Chapter 1 206

Illustration Credits 207

About the Author 208

Select Index 209

Appreciations

A great book on a great subject! It considers time, space, life and God from a biblical perspective while engaging with an atheistic viewpoint. It is evangelistic in tone, and replete with apologetic arguments for the reasonableness of biblical faith, which will strengthen the faith of believers and give food for thought to those thinking about these issues.

Communicating the gospel clearly and winsomely, each chapter has bite-size subsections giving reasons for having faith in the Word of God. Preachers will find the apt quotations from both Christians and non-Christians especially helpful.

Get this book! It will strengthen biblical faith in its case for the God who created time, space and life, and who has revealed himself so we can know him. Those who oppose a biblical view of the subjects are dealt with graciously and fairly, and it can be given evangelistically to anyone prepared to think about the issues raised.

This reviewer found his heart warmed, his faith strengthened, his mind enlarged, his evangelistic zeal stirred and his hope of heaven increased.

—**Steve Carter, MA**, *Retired pastor of Bethel Baptist Church, Tredegar*

'Can someone be a scientist and still believe in a creator God?' is amazingly a question still asked by many today.

This latest little book from Nigel Faithfull (a scientist who believes!) is a real gem! I remember having discussions with him a couple of years ago as to what were 'time' and 'space', we then got on to life, God, the universe ... and everything! I suggested Nigel write a book on these subjects—and here it is!

Reading the manuscript whilst on holiday has been a joy to my mind and to my heart also. Nigel treats his subject thoroughly but in such a way as to engage all types of readers. Whilst experts can be helped, the non-scientific reader is by no means left behind. In each of the sections, following a detailed examination of the subject, the reader is confronted with the all-pervading glory and real-

Appreciations

ity of God himself, building to a final chapter on that very Being.

I heartily commend this book for all to read and pass on to others too.

—**Dr. Andy Christofides,** *Pastor St Mellons Baptist Church Cardiff, author of Day One's 'Lifeline' (2012), and 'Evidence for God' (2010)*

The author has produced an interesting and wide-ranging book looking at the subjects of time, space, life and their relationship to God. Although written from a Bible-based Christian viewpoint, Dr. Faithfull has however sought to be fair and courteous in his dealing with contradictory views. I found a lot of interesting and for me previously unknown facts and figures about the universe and our place in it, but was also reminded of other things that I have forgotten over the years. For a Christian preacher, here is a host of illustrations and quotes, but also for an atheist or agnostic there is plenty to think about. I recommend you make some space on your bookshelf and find time to read it. It will enrich your spiritual life and can deepen your experience of the God who has made all things well.

—**Dr. Chris Pegington,** *Retired pastor of Ebenezer Evangelical Church, Cwmbran, and author of 'A Beginner's Guide to Creation'*

This book is a page-turner, so easy to read. It is informative, revealing some truths you have never heard of, truths that will amaze you. It is inspiring, delivering you from sterile materialism. It is kindly and pastoral and so enormously helpful not only for beginners but for those who have professed to be disciples of Jesus Christ for many years. Take it and read it! Yes! Take it and read it!

—**Dr. Geoff Thomas,** *Pastor Emeritus of Alfred Place Baptist Church, Aberystwyth, Wales (From the Foreword)*

Acknowledgements

I would like to acknowledge some of those who have played a part in the production of this book and been encouragements and an inspiration to me along the way.

Dr. Geoff Thomas has been a pastor, counsellor and friend from 1965, when I came to Aberystwyth as a student. His sermons consistently proclaim God's glory in creation, from the greatest galaxies to the smallest atoms, but above all in the grace to be found in Jesus Christ.

From 2010, when we moved to South Wales, Dr. Andy Christofides has taken over the role of pastor and encourager. Originally trained as a scientist, he is also an amateur astronomer who sees God's design and upholding power displayed in the heavens and on Earth, and often passes on his enthusiasm to the congregation.

Dr. Chris Pegington has been a friend from student days. With a PhD in genetics and further research at Cambridge, he was called to full-time Christian ministry, with several pastorates and periods of missionary work in Austria. He has consistently advocated the Genesis account of creation rather than the Darwinian Theory as universally taught in academia.

Steven Carter, my brother-in-law, has made helpful comments and been able to read the draft manuscript with both a pastoral eye, and with the experience of one originally trained in the printing industry.

Special thanks go to Jim Holmes who has put in many hours of editorial work, transforming the draft manuscript into an attractive publication.

The staff of Newport Museum have been particularly helpful to me on my several visits there to see the artefacts connected with W. H. Davies.

Finally, thanks go to my wife, Eileen, for her patience while I spent hours in front of a computer screen, or at other times seemed miles, or even light-years away in deep thought. I am now back to Earth—almost!

Foreword

The opening words of the Bible are the most well-known sentence of the entire Scripture, words known and quoted all over the world. The words are, "In the beginning God created the heavens and the earth."—especially the earth, our own planet. This world was the special focus of God's creation. That is the meaning and affirmation of the opening words of the Bible.

In our schools and through the media we have all been made aware that our earth, considered in terms of size, is an average sized planet encircling the sun. The earth is dwarfed by the size of four of the other planets, Jupiter, Saturn, Uranus and Neptune, which are all gas giants. Neptune is, in fact, 318 times bigger than planet earth, and yet it is not Neptune but the earth that is the focus of God's attention. Then consider our sun which is a part of great galaxy of similar suns, and this galaxy is called, of course, the Milky Way. Nobody knows how many stars or suns there are in the Milky Way; estimates range from sixty billion to perhaps four hundred billion stars in the Milky Way.

The Hubble telescope has so far detected 80 billion other galaxies in the universe—so it is not hyperbole to compare the number of planets in the universe to the number of grains of sand on the seashore. Yet Genesis chapter one and verse one says that in the beginning God created the heavens and that he particularly created the earth. God has given man a geocentric view of reality. God's interest was focused on our world and its inhabitants, the men and women whom he made in his own image. The rest of Genesis chapter one, and the remainder of the Bible, concentrates on this unique planet of ours, home to the only living people in the whole universe as far as we know, and Scripture looks at the rest of the cosmos as the backcloth to ourselves who can know who we are in relation to God as we are made in his likeness. We inhabit a divinely created world which has been planned, and tested, and spoken to and visited by God's angels and by God the Son.

Such a geocentric view of reality is deplored by many non-Christian intellectuals today. Carl Sagan, the American astronomer who steadily opposed the Christian view of creation, was interviewed in 1996 on the US TV program *Dateline* by Ted Koppel. That interview was to be only a few days before Sagan's death, though Sagan didn't know that he had less than a week to live. Koppel asked him if he had any closing remarks, any words of wisdom he would like to share with the people of the earth, and this is what he said: "We live on a hunk of rock and metal that circles a humdrum star that is one of 400 billion other stars that make up the Milky Way galaxy which is one of billions of other galaxies which make up the universe which may be one of a very large number, perhaps an infinite number of other universes. That is a perspective on human life and our culture that is well worth pondering." Those were his closing despairing words. They are saying this:

We came from nowhere.
We are going nowhere.
There is no purpose in anything that we see around us.
'Life' is meaningless.
Humans are not special in any sense.

How different is the perspective of Genesis chapter one.

There is a Creator.
Mankind has a Maker.
God designed the universe with the world at its heart.
He especially made the earth amongst all the billions of stars in the cosmos.
Humans are very special, made in his image.
Our maker is not silent but speaks to us by his servants and his Son.

When you believe that, then you have a very different outlook on life. You say that the lives of men and women count in the sight of God their Creator and Judge, and they had better humbly know him and do his will. So our world is being confronted by two opposing world views.

What about living creatures on other planets? There have been

Foreword

many amusing, mysterious and persuasive stories to the effect that aliens have come to this earth from other planets. 'The Martians have landed!' is the cry of science fiction. Such aliens are alleged to have built the pyramids, made corn circles in Wiltshire, and frightened sheep farmers in Snowdonia as they were driving along on their quad bikes. These aliens from outer space travel in flying saucers, so it is alleged. Millions will take seriously and reverently fiction like that who yet will never consider the claims of Genesis chapter one or of the life of Jesus of Nazareth. People without God feel terribly alone in this immense universe. They are afraid because they have no hope; rejecting our divine Saviour they begin their forlorn quest for companionship with mythical spacemen.

There is no evidence whatsoever that any other living creatures exist in the entire universe except ourselves on this planet. The nearest planet which has the conditions for possibly having life in it lies outside our solar system, though it is within the Milky Way. It is 200 light years away. You know that light travels at 186 thousand miles in a second; two seconds and you've reached the moon, and yet it would take two centuries travelling at that speed to reach the nearest planet outside the solar system which might have oxygen and water and 'friendly' gravity.

If you are searching for a reason for your existence—and you should—and the explanation for mankind's incredible achievements, his spirit of self sacrifice and creativity, and also why the world is in the state which it's in, then you must read the opening chapters of Genesis. The New Testament is fascinated with the book of Genesis. It refers to it about two hundred times and half of those references are to the first eleven chapters of Genesis. The Lord Jesus Christ quoted or referred to each of the first seven chapters of Genesis.

So the challenge of the Bible is the facticity of the opening ten words with which the Bible begins, the most widely read words in all literature. If you really believe that they are truth, then I think you will have little difficulty in believing the rest of God's word. These words are the end of *atheism*; "God was in the beginning," they affirm. They deny the *polytheism* of Hinduism and its many gods. There is one God alone. They refute the *pantheism* of the New Age movement which makes everything we see to be god. They blow to pieces the theory of *dualism*, that there are two gods, one good and one evil, at war with one another. These words challenge *humanism* because they enthrone God as King of the universe, not man. This God of Genesis chapter one is the living God, and so let us worship and adore him; let us make it our chief end to glorify him and enjoy him for ever.

My dear friend, Dr. Nigel Faithfull, has written this book to help you to understand the truthfulness of the God who created the cosmos and has spoken to us in the Bible. We have been friends for over fifty years during which time I have grown in admiration and respect and affection for him, for his humility, modesty and graciousness. It has been my very great pleasure to read his writings. This book is a page-turner, so easy to read. It is informative, revealing some truths you have never heard of, truths that will amaze you. It is inspiring, delivering you from sterile materialism. It is kindly and pastoral and so enormously helpful not only for beginners but for those who have professed to be disciples of Jesus Christ for many years. Take it and read it! Yes! Take it and read it!

Geoff Thomas
Pastor Emeritus of Alfred Place Baptist Church,
Aberystwyth, Wales

Introduction

We are living in an information age, with universities having departments of information studies, and communications are through the 'information superhighway'. In the UK, the Office for National Statistics in Newport monitors every conceivable aspect of the British economy, population and society, and conducts the ten-yearly census. Internet resources, such as Wikipedia, give instant access to knowledge which researchers could only have dreamed about fifty years ago. The media bombards us with the latest news of space exploration, fossil discoveries, and advances in medical science and genetics. It is a struggle to process all this data and make some sense of it so that it relates to our worldview. At the end of the day we probably just try to keep up our daily routine and leave the universe to sort itself out with the help of the experts. We stoically carry on regardless, with our head in the sand like the ostrich.

This may work for a while, but it leaves a deep sense of hollowness—a vague awareness that we are lacking something. Will we exit the stage of our lives having missed out on finding the purpose for our existence and the meaning behind our wonderful universe? Hopefully this book will begin to open your eyes to the fact that there is a God who designed everything, and intended to have a personal and loving relationship with you.

I began taking an interest in experimental science from the age of about three years, when I prodded an electric fire with an ornamental candle to see what would happen. In God's providence my mother checked up on me just as the flames were spreading. She wrapped me in a rug and smothered the flames of the burning carpet and cushion. Years later my main scientific interest was concerned with the use of flames in spectroscopy for chemical analysis. While growing up, I collected scientific apparatus and chemicals to furnish a home laboratory, but although it was an absorbing interest, there was still a missing dimension to life. I was raised in a Christian home and knew about God, but I had not yet discovered for myself what was needed to make life truly satisfying. I had not yet made sense of God or his universe.

Introduction

All that changed when God revealed himself to me. He showed me that I was a sinful person who had lived a self-absorbed existence. I saw that Jesus Christ had come to this planet to die for me and all who trust him to be their Saviour. The Holy Spirit renewed me inwardly, and opened my eyes to see how the whole magnificent and beautiful universe around me had been designed, and is being upheld, by God. He is the Director of all of history, and at the end of time will come again to judge and renew the world. He also made it clear to me before I went to read chemistry at Aberystwyth University that I should aim to be involved with the chemical analysis of plants and soils. That came true in quite a remarkable way, so I had no doubt it was God's will for me.

Whether your calling is scientific, connected with the arts or social studies, or one of the many other useful trades and professions, hopefully this book will help you come to see the part you can play in the grand scheme of all things. The general thrust of television programmes, school curricula and presentations in museums is that we are here because of a 'Big Bang' and chance evolution over millions of years. That is a cold and miserable scenario and not one which is accepted by all secular scientists. To believe in a Creator God is not being feeble-minded when some of the greatest scientists have done so, such as Isaac Newton, Michael Faraday and James Clerk Maxwell.

This book is for those with an enquiring mind, but not necessarily experts in any particular discipline. The various references may serve as starting points for further research in areas of specific interest. We will look at the basic properties of matter, time and space, and how they affect our lives. The conundrum of the origin of life and its meaning will be dealt with in an historical context, with reference to the emergence of eugenics from the soil of Darwinian evolution. Finally, we try to humbly consider the being and nature of God. Throughout the whole book I have attempted to interpret our observations on the universe, life and faith in the light of the Scriptures, which are the only source of objective truth on origins available to us, and which enable us to

avoid merely human speculations.
To God be all the glory.
Nigel Faithfull
Newport, Wales, November 2017

1

TIME

*Thy time is now and evermore,
Thy place is everywhere.*

John Mason (c. 1646–1694)

1: Time

The elusive entity

Time is like God — we know it exists, it is invisible, and it has to be taken seriously. When we were five years old, we lived each day for the moment, jumping from one experience to another. At ten years of age, we began to think ahead about entering a new school. Life seemed to stretch out endlessly beyond us into the far distance. At fifteen, it seemed like an age before we will be able to learn to drive a car; and as a fresher at university, it seemed like a great while before the final graduation day. Young people imagine they will live for ever, but that is just a vain hope. Time, however, is flying by. The old Roman poet Virgil (70–19BC) coined the Latin phrase *Tempus fugit* (time flies), and it has appeared on sundials and clock faces ever since.

TEMPUS FUGIT: TIME FLIES

W. H. Davies

Time to pause

In all the hustle and rushing about of twenty-first-century life, many endure the long commute to work and return home late at night just in time to kiss the children good night. Then there is the school run, with long waits in the busy traffic, perhaps grabbing time in the evening for a visit to the gym or a rare meal out, or back to school again for a parents' and teachers' evening; surely we need to stop and stand still for a while, take stock of our lives and get a proper perspective on life itself. Where are we going?

W. H. Davies

The Newport-born poet, W. H. Davies (1871–1940), nicknamed the 'Supertramp', wrote the well-loved lines of the poem *Leisure*, often learned in junior school as an introduction to poetry. He had the wisdom to stop and appreciate his environment—but it is doubtful if he found the true answer to the real purpose of life. The longcase clock presented to him by the citizens of Newport is housed in Newport museum. It would have reminded him continually of the passing of time, and the need to find an answer to what will follow when our time on earth shall come to an end.

LEISURE

WHAT is this life if, full of care,
We have no time to stand and stare? —
No time to stand beneath the boughs,
And stare as long as sheep and cows:
No time to see, when woods we pass,
Where squirrels hide their nuts in grass:
No time to see, in broad daylight,
Streams full of stars, like skies at night:
No time to turn at Beauty's glance,
And watch her feet, how they can dance:
No time to wait till her mouth can
Enrich that smile her eyes began?
A poor life this if, full of care,
We have no time to stand and stare.

1: Time

It is not only the younger generation who carry on living regardless that the sand in the upper chamber of the hourglass of their lives is trickling away, slowly but surely, and will all too soon fill the lower bulb, when their time on this planet will have come to an end. This is the solemn thought that inspired Anne Cousin (1824–1906) to pen the hymn *The sands of time are sinking*, and this book will hopefully bring the reader to the same hope of eternal life as she experienced.

The silent stalker

Youth gives way to middle age, and on reaching the age of 50 one finds that one has only to wait a tenth of a lifetime to reach 55, which rapidly shoots by, whereas it would be a whole lifetime to a five-year old. This is because our awareness of the amount of elapsed time is arrived at by comparing the period with our lifespan up to that point. The end result is that our later years, which become occupied with many family and social duties, really seem to pass by at an accelerating rate. We have used the expression *seems* on several occasions. This is because although the length of each day of our lives is still 24 hours, our experience of the passing of time does really change. Time passes silently, and the end of time for each of us will inevitably be death.

Spectators at the Lord's cricket ground who wish to see which direction the wind is coming from will look to the weather vane. There they will see Father Time removing the bails after 'time' is called at the end of the match. He is carrying an hourglass and a scythe, the latter symbolically reaping mortals from the land of the living into the place of the dead. He is the Grim Reaper, and death is something we must all face and deal with.[1] The believer in the God of the Bible, however, knows that there is good news—God has dealt with the problem of death in the death of his dear Son, and how that is possible will be more fully dealt with under *Man's mortality* later in this chapter and elsewhere.

Time is of the essence

Without doubt, our lives are inseparably tied up with time. All we do and think depends on the passage of time, and we cannot escape from the time-space continuum in which we exist. Authors have fantasised about the possibility of travelling in time. H. G. Wells (1866–1946) published his novel *The Time Machine* in 1895. He conceived a machine capable of travelling millions of years into the future, but he could only envisage a degenerate and menacing world at the end of the journey. He rejected the Christian

---

[1] http://www.evangelical-times.org/archive/item/7534/Biblical-theological/Time-is-of-the-essence/

message as one which didn't work for him, yet he would have found there the hope which he sought in vain elsewhere.

H G WELLS CONCEIVED A MACHINE TRAVELLING MILLIONS OF YEARS INTO THE FUTURE . . . TO A DEGENERATE AND MENACING WORLD.

H. G. Wells

The author J. B. Priestley (1894–1984) quipped that he (Wells) had sold his birthright for 'a pot of message'. Priestley himself was fascinated by the nature of time, co-authoring *Time Alive* with J. W. Dunne in 1957, and *Man and Time* in 1964. He speculated about pre-cognitive dreaming and whether time could alter to allow this. Priestley also became convinced that the soul would survive after death, probably in another kind of time.[2] He hoped religion could help unify the quarrelling nations, postulating, 'just as a first step, we can at least believe that man lives under God in a great mystery.'[3] Just like Wells, however, all he could foresee was 'an age of deepening inner despair and of appalling catastrophes'.

---

[2] Bruce Charlton, *J. B. Priestley and Time*, 15 June 2010, charltonteaching.blogspot.co.uk
[3] J.B. Priestley, *Literature and Western Man*, Heinemann, 1960, pp440-6

A matter of time

The matter we see around us, the soil, trees, rocks and buildings, all depend on time to continue to exist. Time is an essential factor for the existence of the universe and all forms of life. Just think of the structure of atoms—the building blocks of everything we can see. Atoms consist basically of a core of protons and neutrons around which electrons are orbiting (or they can be considered, according to quantum theory, as an electron cloud).

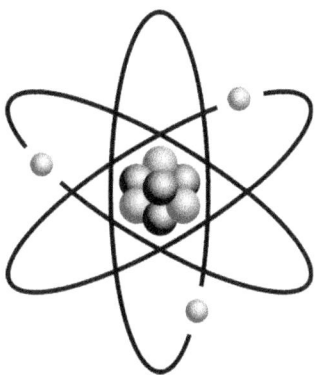

The size of the nucleus is a small fraction of the size of the atom itself, and the electron cloud is really just empty space containing no matter. If time stood still and the electrons stopped orbiting, their negative charge would cause them to crash into the positive nucleus, and the atom would shrink by a factor of 40,000. Its density would become 1,014 times larger than everyday material, and the whole earth would become the size of a pyramid.[4]

There is no scientific reason why electrons should keep in motion other than the fact that God, having created the universe by speaking it into existence, now 'upholds the universe by the word of his power' (Heb. 1:3). Joseph Priestley (1733–1804), the acknowledged discoverer of oxygen, in considering the nature of matter wrote:

> It is impossible to conceive that any one atom should approach another without a *foreign power*, viz. that of the deity; and therefore bodies consisting of such atoms could not hold together, so as to constitute *compact substances*, without this constant agency.[5]

---

[4] Image http://old.iupac.org/didac/Didac%20Eng/Didac03/Content/M03%20-%20M04.htm

[5] Joseph Priestley, *Disquisitions Relating to Matter and Spirit*, 2nd Edn., J. Johnson, Birmingham, 1782, p40

1: Time

> BACK TO THE FUTURE DAY . . . WHERE SEVERAL TECHNOLOGICAL PREDICTIONS WERE SEEN TO HAVE BEEN INVENTED, BUT OTHERS YET TO BE SEEN.

Time in view

The BBC's *Dr Who* is the longest running TV sci-fi show in the world. It was launched on 23 November, 1963, the day after the assassination of President J. F. Kennedy, and it continues in autumn 2018 as series 11, featuring the first ever female Doctor. The various adventures involve travelling through time in a time-machine called a TARDIS (Time And Relative Dimensions In Space), which is disguised as a police call-box. From 5–14 million people in the UK alone have regularly tuned in to allow their imaginations to experience this exciting but fictitious time-travel.

In the cinema, the *Back to the Future* trilogy has been popular with releases in 1985, 1989, and 1990. Again, time travel is involved, but in a DeLorean car converted for this purpose by Doc Brown who shares his adventures with the young man Marty McFly. Time travel was more modest than with Wells, so we only get to 1955, 2015 and 1885 respectively in the trilogy. Some time ago, 21st October 2015 was celebrated as 'Back to the Future Day' when several technological predictions were seen to have been subsequently invented, but others are yet to be seen.

Whatever the media may say, we remain trapped in time and when the program or film is finished, or the final page is read, the whole experience has been escapism into a fantasy world. Nevertheless, we remain fascinated by time and feel we want to understand it better.

1: Time

WHATEVER THE MEDIA MAY SAY, WE REMAIN TRAPPED IN TIME AND WHEN THE PROGRAM OR FILM IS FINISHED, OR THE FINAL PAGE IS READ, THE WHOLE EXPERIENCE HAS BEEN ESCAPISM INTO A FANTASY WORLD.

William Shakespeare

Time to talk

Our language is replete with expressions relating to time. 'Time and tide wait for no man', 'no time like the present', and 'his time was up' are a few examples. We often talk about having either 'time on our hands', or conversely, 'no time to do anything'. Yet although we often mention time, do we really know what time is?

William Shakespeare (1564–1616) wasn't into time travel machines, but he felt the despair at being in a time-limited existence. In *As You Like It* he compared the world to a stage on

1: Time

which we play out our lives in seven acts. In the first we begin as a puking infant, and in the 'last scene of all, that ends this strange eventful history, is second childishness and mere oblivion, sans teeth, sans eyes, sans taste, sans everything.' Is that it? Dementia and oblivion?

> 'ALL THE WORLD'S A STAGE,
> AND ALL THE MEN AND WOMEN MERELY PLAYERS;
> THEY HAVE THEIR EXITS AND THEIR ENTRANCES;
> AND ONE MAN IN HIS TIME PLAYS MANY PARTS,
> HIS ACTS BEING SEVEN AGES.'
>
> ~ WILLIAM SHAKESPEARE ~

The wisest man who ever lived was probably King Solomon. He was one of the richest in the world at that time. He had it all, but still was not satisfied, so he set about trying to discover what made people happy. He would leave God and religion out of the equation so as not to complicate the issue. He would impartially look at what people did 'under the sun', in the space-time dimension of planet earth. He considered all the beautiful houses with their parks and gardens, lakes and arboretums, liveried servants and attractive maidservants, lavish entertainment and all the amassed silver and gold. Surely this is the ultimate goal of our own age of materialism? Yet his conclusion is shocking:

> So I hated life, because what is done under the sun was grievous to me, for all is vanity and a striving after wind. I hated all my toil in which I toil under the sun, seeing that I must leave it to the man who will come after me, and who knows whether he will be wise or a fool? Yet he will be master of all for which I toiled and used my wisdom under the sun. This also is vanity. (Ecclesiastes 2:17–19)

There's the rub—he could take nothing with him beyond the grave, and his successor could squander all these hard-earned assets. He reckoned that 'it is good and proper for a man to eat and drink, and to find satisfaction in his toilsome labour under the sun during the few days of life God has given him' (Ecclesiastes 5:18). Life is short, and by the end of his book Solomon looks beyond the sun to find some meaning to his brief existence: 'Remember also your Creator in the days of your youth, before the evil days come and the years draw near of which you will say, "I have no pleasure in them"'(Ecclesiastes 12:1).

LIFE IS SHORT, AND BY THE END OF HIS BOOK SOLOMON LOOKS BEYOND THE SUN TO FIND SOME MEANING TO HIS BRIEF EXISTENCE: 'REMEMBER ALSO YOUR CREATOR IN THE DAYS OF YOUR YOUTH . . .'

Science and Time

Isaac Newton

Science is known for giving definite answers, so perhaps it will be able to give us some reliable facts about time. The most famous British scientist of all time has to be Sir Isaac Newton (1642–1727). Skip over the maths if you like, but it is included to show how his mind worked, and how he revealed the order inherent in the functioning of the universe. He is most noted for formulating his three Laws of Motion, which form the basis of classical mechanics. They deal with inertia, acceleration, and action and reaction. Most people remember his 'discovery' of gravity, but more particularly the Universal Law of Gravitation. This law is expressed by the formula:

$F = G\frac{mM}{r^2}$, where $G = 6.67 \times 10^{-11}$ N-m²/kg² and F is the force of attraction; G is the gravitational constant; m and M are the first and second masses, and r is the distance between the centres of masses. In practical calculations, m is usually the mass of a relatively small object when compared to M, which stands for the mass of the earth.

Now the force due to gravity is:

$F = mg$, where m is the mass of the body and g is the acceleration due to gravity.

Combining the two equations we get:

$$mg = G\frac{mM}{r^2} \text{ or } g = G\frac{M}{r^2}$$

On earth the acceleration due to gravity is 9.8 m/s², where m is in metres and s is the time in seconds, and any effect of friction from air resistance is ignored.

Using these laws, which together form the basis of that branch of astronomy called *celestial mechanics*, Newton was able to explain the motion of the planets, and all involve the time factor. Time was an inescapable property of the universe as seen by Newton, where all the heavenly bodies moved according to the rules and laws of motion. He writes in his *Scholium* (see below):

> But hitherto I have not been able to discover the cause of those properties of gravity from phaenomena, and I frame no hypotheses. And to us it is enough, that gravity does really exist, and act according to the laws which we have explained, and abundantly serves to account for all the motions of the celestial bodies, and of our sea.

He was not able to discover the cause of the gravity which accounts for all the planetary motions, but he was content to know it did really exist and that God was in control.

NEWTON WAS NOT AN ORTHODOX CHRISTIAN YET HE WAS EMPHATIC REGARDING A DIVINE CREATOR WHO ALSO CONTINUOUSLY SUSTAINED THE CREATION.

1: Time

Newton was not an orthodox Christian (he was more of a deist), yet he was emphatic regarding a divine Creator who also continuously sustained the creation. His major mathematical work was his *Principia (Philosophiae Naturalis Principia Mathematica* (1687)) in which he included a *Scholium* expressing the philosophy behind his scientific reasoning.[6]

NEWTON BELIEVED IN A GOD WHO IS A DIVINE PERSON OF ABSOLUTE POWER, WHO CREATED AN ORDERLY UNIVERSE CAPABLE OF BEING UNDERSTOOD AND GOVERNED BY LAWS WHICH MAY BE SYSTEMATIZED.

This most beautiful System of the Sun, Planets, and Comets, could only proceed from the counsel and dominion of an intelligent and powerful being. And if the fixed Stars are the centres of other like systems, these, being form'd by the like wise counsel, must be all subject to the dominion of One; especially since the light of the fixed Stars is of the same nature with the light of the Sun, and from every system light passes into all the other systems. And lest the systems of the fixed Stars should, by their gravity, fall on each other mutually, he hath placed those Systems at immense distances from one another.

This Being governs all things, not as the soul of the world, but as Lord over all … The supreme God is a Being eternal, infinite, absolutely perfect; but a being, however perfect, without dominion, cannot be said to be Lord God;

---

[6] http://isaac-newton.org/general-%20scholium

for we say, my God, your God, the God of *Israel*, the God of Gods, and Lord of Lords; but we do not say, my Eternal, your Eternal, the Eternal of *Israel*, the Eternal of Gods.

Newton believed in a God who is a divine person of absolute power, who created an orderly universe capable of being understood and governed by laws which may be systematized. These laws could be relied upon to be valid from one day to the next. There is no reason to assume this to be the case unless there was an underlying controlling force. The natural scenario would be to expect a universe characterized by disorder if the Second Law of Thermodynamics has been in operation for the 13.8 billions of years modern cosmologists claim for the age of the universe. It was in 1856 that the German physicist Rudolf Clausius famously stated the Second Law as that the *entropy of the universe tends to a maximum*, in other words, the disorder of the universe is always increasing. Even Aristotle (384–322BC) was aware of this general erosion caused by time: 'Time crumbles things; everything grows old under the power of time and is forgotten through the lapse of time.' The further we go into time, the more run-down and chaotic the universe as a whole becomes. Science up to the end of the nineteenth century has offered us no hope for the control of time or slowing down its passage, and certainly no way to escape from its effects altogether.

Relativity and time

A significant step in the scientific understanding of the nature of time and its relationship to space was proposed by Albert Einstein (1879–1955). Up to this time, both the properties of time and dimension had been considered as fixed values. Post-Newton man could leave God out of the equation and have faith in these absolute values. The scientific elite were in control of the facts of life and the physical universe and politicians and sociologists should act accordingly. Charles Darwin (1809–1882) had published *On the Origin of Species by Means of Natural Selection, or the Preservation of Favoured Races in the Struggle for Life* in 1859 which was another

1: Time

attempt to leave God out of the reckoning concerning origins and give man his autonomy. The full title of the *Origin of Species* given above betrays the arrogance of those who devalue other ethnic groups other than their own which eventually led to the horrors of the Nazi holocaust. God's word declares all people as equal in value and dignity before him, and much bloodshed would have been avoided if those with high opinions of their 'scientific' theories had founded them on God's revelation.

In 1905, Einstein published his Theory of Special Relativity regarding the relationship of space and time. The same year he established the mass-energy equivalence expressed later by the well-known formula, $E = mc^2$, where E is the energy of an object of mass 'm' and 'c' is the speed of light. Later, between 1907 and 1915, Einstein proposed his Theory of General Relativity, which is a theory of gravitation. According to general relativity, the observed gravitational attraction between masses results from the warping of space and time by those masses. Thus the same object could have different lengths, and the same event could take place at two different times when applying his theory to two different observers who were moving with respect to each other. This effect could be calculated, but the inability to state a fixed value for space and time was unsettling to scientists who liked to say they could be relied on to provide unalterable statements of truth by employing their scientific methods.

Time travel?

Einstein's relativity theories established that as one travelled closer to the speed of light (about 300,000 km per second), the time on a watch on that person, and even his body clock, would appear to run slower to a stationary observer. However, to the traveller, time would appear to be passing at the normal rate. If the traveller returned to earth, he would have aged less than the observer. Realistically, one could never travel at such high speeds, and at lower speeds we are talking in terms of fractions of a second. The effect of relativity is real, but will make no practical difference to our lifespan, and the possibility of exceeding the speed of light and travelling backwards in time has been disproved.[7]

Einstein and God

Einstein stated in a letter in 1954,

> I do not believe in a personal God and I have never denied this but have expressed it clearly. If something is in me which can be called religious, then it is the unbounded admiration for the structure of the world so far as our science can reveal.

He described himself as either agnostic, or pantheistic like Spinoza, content to worship the wonderful universe around him and his own ability to make sense of it. He considered biblical Christianity as childish superstition, and was glad to be free of its shackles and the demands of 'a God who rewards and punishes his creatures, or has a will of the type of which we are conscious in ourselves. An individual who should survive his physical death is

---

[7] http://www.emc2-explained.info/Time-Dilation/#.VhdgqTZdG-o

1: Time

also beyond my comprehension, nor do I wish it otherwise; such notions are for the fears or absurd egoism of feeble souls.'[8]

Einstein had even rejected Newton's cautious belief in God. Newton believed in a personal God, but Einstein said, 'Teachers of religion must have the stature to give up the doctrine of a personal God ... they will have to avail themselves of those forces which are capable of cultivating the Good, the True, and the Beautiful in humanity itself.'[9]

EINSTEIN LEAVES US WITH A WONDERFUL BUT EMPTY AND LONELY UNIVERSE.

Einstein leaves us with a wonderful but empty and lonely universe. This same atheistic scientific humanism led Bertrand Russell (1872–1970) to declare, 'I believe that when I die I shall rot, and nothing of my ego will survive.' Surely there is more meaning to life, and a better hope than this? Herman Hupfeld (1894–1951) the American songwriter, remembered for his song *As Time Goes By* (1931), would seem to agree in his lyrics for this song, the latter part of which was famously used in *Casablanca* (1942), that Einstein's ideas lead to worry and apprehension:

'I BELIEVE THAT WHEN I DIE I SHALL ROT, AND NOTHING OF MY EGO WILL SURVIVE.'

~ BERTRAND RUSSELL ~

---

[8] https://en.wikipedia.org/wiki/Religious_views_of_Albert_Einstein
[9] *Science, Philosophy and Religion*, a Symposium, New York, 1941

AS TIME GOES BY [10]

This day and age we're living in
Gives cause for apprehension
With speed and new invention
And things like fourth dimension.
Yet we get a trifle weary
With Mr. Einstein's theory.
So we must get down to earth at times
Relax relieve the tension

And no matter what the progress
Or what may yet be proved
The simple facts of life are such
They cannot be removed.

You must remember this
A kiss is just a kiss, a sigh is just a sigh.
The fundamental things apply
As time goes by ...

Uncertainty

Following shortly after Einstein's Theory of General Relativity, the German physicist Werner Heisenberg (1901–1976) proposed, in 1927, that the more precisely the position of some particle (like an electron) is determined, the less precisely its momentum can be known, and vice versa. Even if one could determine the position of an electron at a certain time, there would be no way of predicting where it would be in the future. The best one could hope for would be to calculate a probability that the electron would be present at a given time. This discovery became known as Heisenberg's Uncertainty Principle. Man would never be able to discover

---

[10] http://letras.mus.br/natalie-cole/809251/

1: Time

the behaviour of an electron in time and space without influencing that behaviour. The uncertainty principle also applies to quantum mechanics. On an atomic particle level, objective truth regarding time and space has slipped from our grasp.

The last century
It is now over a century since Albert Einstein published the *Annus mirabilis* papers in the *Annalen der Physik* scientific journal in 1905. These four articles led to the foundation of modern physics and changed views on space, time, mass, and energy. But have these ideas on the nature of space and time made any lasting difference as to how we live, or improved our view of the purpose of life? Do we value time any more than our predecessors?

Time passes and is gone for ever
Thomas Edison (1847–1931) was an American scientific genius who published 1,368 patents and invented the phonograph and the first commercially viable light bulb. He advised, 'Time is not a commodity that can be stored for future use. It must be invested hour by hour, or else it is gone for ever.'[11]

Rather as in Einstein's case, Nature was Edison's god, the Supreme intelligence that rules matter.

---

[11] http://www.quoteyard.com/quotes/time/page/3/

> 'THE PROBLEM WITH GETTING EVERYTHING IS YOU RUN OUT OF REASONS TO KEEP TRYING . . .'
>
> ~ MARKUS PERSSON ~

In 2014, Markus Persson (born 1979) sold his Minecraft video game to Microsoft for £1.2bn. You would think he would feel liberated with so many possibilities to occupy his time, but that is not the case. Firstly he became bored with life and wasting his time, tweeting the following:

> In Sweden, I will sit around … watching my reflection in the monitor (tweet of 29 August 2015).

Secondly he lost, at least to start with, the incentive to persevere with his skills, stating:

> The problem with getting everything is you run out of reasons to keep trying, and human interaction becomes impossible due to imbalance.

Someone sent him the tweet, 'without God, the imbalance remains forever. People spend their entire lives searching for the thing to fill that void. Find God...' Persson replied that 'god is a made up mental crutch designed to fill that void, so you're absolutely right.'

> 'I WAS HOLDING A GOLD STATUE AND I WAS THE LONELIEST I HAD EVER BEEN.'
>
> ~ NICOLE KIDMAN ~

1: Time

The 2002 Oscar-winning actress Nicole Kidman (born 1967) said, 'I was holding a gold statue and I was the loneliest I had ever been' (Daily Telegraph, 10 October 2015, p3). We would argue that nothing man has ever designed can fill that inner void and longing for meaning, and that far from being a crutch, the God revealed in the Bible presents not only a personal relationship, but also a challenge which has led many to martyrdom, even in recent times.

We are not surprised that great scientific minds do not, or will not, accept that there is a personal God who wants a relationship with them. It is a matter of the hearts of men and women being prejudiced against God from birth as a result of the fall, yet they have to admit that there is a remarkable order in the universe that is opposed to the natural tendency to disorder. This order permits scientific investigation and the establishment of laws and patterns of action which they define as Nature, the personification of their god.

The Apostle Paul discerned this tendency in his own day nearly 2,000 years ago. He wrote in Romans 1:20–23:

> For his invisible attributes, namely, his eternal power and divine nature, have been clearly perceived, ever since the creation of the world, in the things that have been made. So they are without excuse. For although they knew God … they became futile in their thinking, and exchanged the glory of the immortal God for images resembling mortal man and birds and animals and creeping things.

'FOR HIS INVISIBLE ATTRIBUTES, NAMELY, HIS ETERNAL POWER AND DIVINE NATURE HAVE BEEN CLEARLY PERCEIVED, EVER SINCE THE CREATION OF THE WORLD, IN THE THINGS THAT HAVE BEEN MADE.'

~ THE APOSTLE PAUL ~

Have we been prejudiced against a personal Creator God and merely repeated the views of scientists who have attributed to Nature the power which could only belong to an all-powerful Being distinct from our universe. They have adopted such views to try and wriggle out of the need to give an account of themselves, and their lives and actions, to such a God. To have to do so would remove the seat of authority from their own hearts to that of God's revealed will in the Bible, which they are reluctant to do.

1: Time

Some scientists who did believe in God

Einstein thought it feeble-minded to believe in the gospel of Jesus Christ. Ironically, out of his three scientific heroes whose portraits graced the wall of his study, two were evangelical Christians: Michael Faraday and James Clerk Maxwell.

FARADAY CLAIMS TO HAVE BEEN TAUGHT TO THINK BY A BOOK BY ISAAC WATTS 'THE IMPROVEMENT OF THE MIND'.

Michael Faraday (1791–1867) [12] [13]

Michael Faraday was born on 22 September 1791 at Newington Butts, now in the London Borough of Southwark, where his father was trading as a blacksmith. Michael earned a little money delivering Sunday newspapers before his family went to church. He did this so conscientiously that his employer, who ran a booksell-

---

[12] J. H. Gladstone, *Michael Faraday*, Macmillan, London, 1874; https://ia700400.us.archive.org/20/items/michaelfaraday00gladuoft/michaelfaraday00gladuoft.pdf

[13] Bence Jones, *The Life and Letters of Faraday*, Vols. 1 & 2, Longmans, Green & Co., London, 1870; https://archive.org/details/b21929622_0001 and https://archive.org/details/b21929622_0002

ing and binding business, took him on for seven years as an apprentice from 1805–1812.

As books came in for binding, his naturally inquisitive mind was fed by reading the various articles, such as the section on *Electricity* in the *Encyclopaedia Britannica*. He also read Jane Marcet's *Conversations in Chemistry*. He claims to have been taught to think by Isaac Watts' (1674–1748) *The Improvement of the Mind*. This last book, written from a biblical perspective, structured his future method of working. Watts says, 'Let the hope of new discoveries, as well as the satisfaction and pleasures of known truths, animate your daily industry.'

'LET THE HOPE OF NEW DISCOVERIES, AS WELL AS THE SATISFACTION AND PLEASURES OF KNOWN TRUTHS, ANIMATE YOUR DAILY INDUSTRY.'

~ ISAAC WATTS ~

Faraday's church

Faraday's parents brought him up in the Sandemanian tradition. This was founded by John Glas (1695–1773) and carried forward by his son-in-law Robert Sandeman (1718–1771). They believed in separation of the church from state control and aimed to implement the spirituality of the church in apostolic times. In 1821, a month after his marriage to Sarah, he made his confession of sin and profession of faith before the church. Sarah asked why he didn't give any warning of his intention, but he replied simply 'that is between me and my God.' He was elected an elder in 1840, and preached alternate Sundays.

Faraday's Creator God

Faraday believed that the conclusions from scientific experiments should be unaffected by one's religion. Thus, when, on 26 February 1849, Prince Albert visited the Institution for a private lecture on magnetic bodies, Faraday declared, 'I cannot doubt that a glorious discovery in natural knowledge, and of the wisdom and power of God in the creation, is awaiting our age...' Faraday was dealing with hypotheses which could be verified by experiment and then formulated into laws. The origin of the universe and Darwinian macro-evolution do not come into this category, and therefore *are* influenced by one's religion or world-view.

Faraday's laboratory at the Royal Institution

At another public lecture attended by Prince Albert, Faraday stated, 'I believe that the truth of that future (life) cannot be brought to his knowledge by any exertion of his (man's) mental powers, however exalted they may be; that it is made known to him by other teaching than his own, and is received through simple belief of the testimony given. Even in earthly matters I believe that 'the invisible things of Him from the creation of the world are clearly seen, being understood by the things that are made, even His eternal power and Godhead' (Romans 1:20), which was particularly appropriate as he explored the invisible forces of electricity and magnetism and, for a time, gravity.

Near the end of his life he wrote: 'The thought of death ... brings to the Christian the thought of Him who died, was judged, and who rose again for the justification of those who believe in Him. Though the fear of death be a great thought, the hope of eternal life is a far greater.' As his death approached, he meditated on Psalms 23 and 46, and then on 25 August 1867, while sitting peacefully in his study chair, he passed into the presence of his Lord, the great Creator and the Saviour of all those who will likewise put their trust in Him.

He was a humble man, and refused the offer to be buried alongside Sir Isaac Newton in Westminster Abbey, choosing instead a private burial in unconsecrated ground in Highgate Cemetery.

'THE THOUGHT OF DEATH ... BRINGS TO THE CHRISTIAN THE THOUGHT OF HIM WHO DIED, WAS JUDGED, AND WHO ROSE AGAIN FOR THE JUSTIFICATION OF THOSE WHO BELIEVE IN HIM.'

1: Time

His researches had revealed the principles behind the electric motor, dynamo and transformer, and formulated the two laws of electrolysis, and the two laws of electromagnetic induction. He had discovered that magnetic lines of force emanated into the space around an electric wire through which an electric current was flowing. There did not need to be any means of conduction present in the air for this to happen. This formed the basis for one of Maxwell's famous discoveries—electromagnetic wave theory.

James Clerk Maxwell (1831–1879)[14]

James Clerk Maxwell was Cavendish Professor of Physics at Cambridge University. He was revered by Einstein, who said, 'One scientific epoch ended and another began with James Clerk Maxwell.' When Einstein was asked if he had stood on the shoulders of Newton, he replied: 'No, I stand on Maxwell's shoulders.' Stephen Hawking said, 'Maxwell is the physicist's physicist', and Max Planck recognised that 'He achieved greatness unequalled.'[15]

'YOU MAY SEARCH THE SCRIPTURES AND NOT FIND A TEXT TO STOP YOU IN YOUR EXPLORATIONS...'

~ JAMES CLERK MAXWELL ~

His basis for research was that God had created a structured universe and given man liberty to investigate it without constraint. While an undergraduate at Trinity College, Cambridge, he wrote concerning his God-given mandate for scientific endeavour:

---

[14] Lewis Campbell & William Garnett, *The Life of James Clerk Maxwell*, with Selection from His Correspondence and Occasional Writings, Macmillan, London 1882; available from https://archive.org/details/lifejamesclerkm01garngoog
[15] http://www.famousscientists.org/james-clerk-maxwell/

'nothing was to be left unexamined,' there was to be no 'holy ground' where Christians should not trespass. 'You may fly to the ends of the world and find no God but the Author of Salvation. You may search the Scriptures and not find a text to stop you in your explorations ...' Shortly afterwards he came under conviction of his sin and committed himself to God, trusting Christ for salvation. He wrote: 'I have the capacity of being more wicked than any example that man could set me, and ... if I escape, it is only by God's grace helping me to get rid of myself, partially in science, more completely in society,—but not perfectly except by committing myself to God...' His heart was changed and he became more concerned for the welfare of others. For the next thirteen years he taught Working Men's classes every week and showed his kindness by helping a fellow student suffering with eye-strain by reading to him from a textbook.

Saturn's rings

In 1859 James Clerk Maxwell published *On the Stability of the Motion of Saturn's Rings*. He was awarded the Adams Prize for his essay which contained many pages of detailed mathematical calculations. He discovered how Saturn's rings could remain stable over a long time, neither flying outwards into space nor collapsing down onto Saturn due to  its gravity. Britain's Astronomer Royal, Sir George Biddell Airy, commented: 'It is one of the most remarkable applications of mathematics to physics that I have ever seen.' The Voyager 2 photographs of Saturn taken in 1980 confirmed Maxwell's theory which he formulated over a century earlier.

In 1861 he published *On Physical Lines of Force*, which predicted that there were electromagnetic waves which could travel at the speed of light, followed by his famous equations in 1865, which describe the generation and interaction of electrical and magnetic fields, and showed how they can move through space as waves at the speed of light. They formed a vital bridge between Faraday's laws and Einstein's relativity theory and the later quantum theory. In the late 1880s, Heinrich Hertz (1857–1894) based his discovery of electromagnetic radio waves on Maxwell's theories, and was able to prove for the first time Maxwell's prediction that electromagnetic waves did indeed travel at the speed of light.

MAXWELL TURNED WITH SIMPLE FAITH TO THE GOSPEL OF THE SAVIOUR.

In 1871 Maxwell was pressurised to return from his Scottish estate to Cambridge to direct the construction and equipping of the now famous Cavendish Laboratory, where the electron and neutron were discovered and which inspired twenty-nine Nobel prize-winners. In his sixth year as Cavendish professor, he began to be afflicted with the same fatal illness endured by his mother, abdominal cancer. A minister who visited him in his final weeks witnessed that '... his illness drew out the whole heart and soul and spirit of the man: his firm and undoubting faith in the Incarnation and all its results; in the full sufficiency of the Atonement; in the work of the Holy Spirit. He had gauged and fathomed all the schemes and systems of philosophy, and had found them utterly empty and unsatisfying—"unworkable" was his own word about them—and he turned with simple faith to the Gospel of the Saviour.' He died on 5 November 1879, and was buried in Parton churchyard near Glenlair.

1: Time

Science and time in the 21st century

In December 2008, Professor Brian Cox (born 1968), the well-known BBC TV host of science programmes, presented an edition of *Horizon* entitled *Do you know what time it is?* He said he wanted to find out what makes time tick, did time have a beginning, and what time is it? He is himself the Professor of Particle Physics and Astronomy at Manchester University, so it was a thorough examination of the current knowledge of the subject of time with special reference to Einstein and relativity. Cox asked himself, 'What makes time tick?', 'Is the flow of time an illusion?', 'Did time have a beginning?', 'Does our future already exist?'

'WHAT MAKES TIME TICK?'
'IS THE FLOW OF TIME AN ILLUSION?'
'DID TIME HAVE A BEGINNING?'
'DOES OUR FUTURE ALREADY EXIST?'

Length of day

The programme begins by considering the question 'What time is it?' Time on earth is conveniently related to the length of our day, which is the time it takes for one complete revolution of the earth around its axis. This is about 24 hours, but the effects of the moon on the tides, the friction caused by the air's jet stream and the core-mantle coupling continuously slightly slow the speed of rotation. A modern day is about 1.7 milliseconds longer than it was a century ago, but there is a wobble effect which means some years are slightly shorter than the previous year. A more constant measure of time, Universal Time, is defined by the frequency of microwave radiation from a caesium-133 atom. Excited electrons drop back into a lower energy orbit and emit the excess energy as a radiation vibrating at 9 billion times a second (9,192,631,770Hz). This is called an atomic clock and is the most accurate measure of the passage of time on earth.

'When did time begin?'

We experience everything *now*. The sun, however, is 93 million miles away, so when we see a sunrise or sunset we are looking at light that has taken 8 minutes to reach us. We are not seeing the sun as it is at this very moment. If we look at stars and distant galaxies, this effect is even more pronounced. We are led to ask, 'When did time begin?'

Cox mentioned the Hubble Ultra-Deep Field image of a small region of space in the constellation Fornax, estimated to originate 13 billion years ago. Since making the programme, the image resulting from 10-years' worth of data was released in 2012, known as the Extreme Deep Field, and originating from galaxies 13.2 billion light years away. This is reckoned to be just 450 million years after the so-called 'big bang' event. Cox commented that 'so the theory goes,' it incorporates the idea that time started at the big bang, and that the big bang had no 'yesterday'.

How old is the universe?

The observation of the colour-shift from blue to red of light emitted by supernovae caused by an expanding universe also indicates that space and time apparently originated about 13.7 billion years ago. We would comment that this could be one hypothesis to be drawn from the observed data, but scientists differ as to the nature of this 'big bang event', and creation scientists would also suggest the possibility that the universe could have been instantaneously created *in situ* with an appearance of age.

1: Time

Let there be light!

According to the Bible, God made light, space, time and the earth, complete with vegetation, before he made the sun, moon and stars on the fourth day of creation. In the third verse of the Bible God said, 'Let there be light!' This light would have been in the form of a glow before its source became located mainly in the sun and stars.

> And God made the two great lights—the greater light to rule the day and the lesser light to rule the night—and the stars. And God set them in the expanse of the heavens to give light on the earth, to rule over the day and over the night, and to separate the light from the darkness. And God saw that it was good. And there was evening and there was morning, the fourth day. (Genesis 1:16–19)

God was clearly introducing a regulatory principle over the passage of time on planet earth. There was to be a period for people to work, called day, and a period for resting from work and sleeping, called night. God saw that this arrangement was good, and I think most people would agree with that. God ceased from creating on the seventh day and set it apart as holy or special. This instituted the concept of a week, and later on God also designated one day in seven for people to take a break and hopefully consider their relationship with creation and the God who originated it, which is also the aim of this book.

'AND GOD SET THEM IN THE EXPANSE OF THE HEAVENS TO GIVE LIGHT ON THE EARTH, TO RULE OVER THE DAY AND OVER THE NIGHT, AND TO SEPARATE THE LIGHT FROM THE DARKNESS. AND GOD SAW THAT IT WAS GOOD.'

What caused the universe?

Professor Cox is faced with the question of what triggered the formation of the universe. Where did it come from? If divine revelation is set aside, the theories will be endless and can never be proved. We have a suggestion that another form of universe existed previously which gave rise to our existing universe. Professor Neil Turok (born 1958) Director, Perimeter Institute for Theoretical Physics (Waterloo, Ontario, Canada) has used string theory to suggest there were two parallel worlds called branes (which can have multiple dimensions and where a membrane is a two-dimensional brane). He suggests that two of these time-space branes, which were previously separated by a fourth dimension of space, collided and collapsed at the big bang, space became non-existent and density was infinite. Our present universe exploded outwards from this point and is ever expanding. Turok is still investigating this 'cosmological bounce'.

THE GENESIS ACCOUNT OF THE CREATION OF THE UNIVERSE IS . . . EASY TO UNDERSTAND AND REQUIRES NO COMPLEX MATHEMATICAL MODEL TO EXPLAIN HOW IT GOT HERE.

1: Time

He also writes concerning the universe: 'The presence of dark energy, as well as the extreme simplicity in the large scale structure, seem to me profound clues which no existing theoretical paradigm adequately explains.' We would argue that the Genesis account of the creation of the universe is extremely easy to understand and requires no complex mathematical model to explain how it got here. By leaving God out of our theories, they become inordinately complicated. Yet that is not to say that our greatest minds will not be stretched to their limits in trying to formulate the nature and behaviour of our universe, which is hardly surprising when we realise that its boundless limits must reflect its creation by an infinite God.

What is the smallest time possible?

Perhaps the answer to the nature of time will be found by looking at the smallest time interval possible. This is known as the Planck time. It is the time taken for light to travel, in a vacuum, a distance of 1 Planck length, the shortest imaginable distance. The unit is named after Max Planck, who proposed it, and is about 5.4×10^{-44} seconds. This is largely theoretical, because as of May 2010, the smallest time interval uncertainty in direct measurements is of the order of 12 attoseconds (1.2×10^{-17} seconds), about 2.2×10^{26} Planck times. Putting this another way, the size of the Planck length can be visualized as follows: if a particle or dot about 0.1 mm in size (about the smallest the unaided human eye can see) were magnified to be as large as the observable universe, then inside that universe-sized "dot", the Planck length would be roughly the size of an actual 0.1 mm dot. (ref. wikipedia.org). The time for light to travel across that dot must be unimaginably small, and of no practical significance in aiding our understanding of the nature of time.

'HOW DO WE DEFINE THE TIMELINE OF OUR
LIVES? WHY CAN'T WE STAND STILL IN TIME, AND
WHY DO WE HAVE TO GET OLDER?'

~ BRIAN COX, BBC ~

Our lifetime

The last questions Cox considered were 'How do we define the timeline of our lives? Why can't we stand still in time, and why do we have to get older?' Einstein saw time as a dimension which we move through just like we move through space. It seems to be fixed and unalterable. Although we cannot travel through space at the speed of light, it may be theoretically possible to travel through time at the speed of light.

The time of our lives
If we are standing upon a massively large object (like the world), then time will tick infinitesimally slower at our feet than at the level of our head. A radio signal bounced off Venus back to earth has been shown to be slowed down by 200 microseconds over the return trip because of the effect of passing the huge mass of the sun. This  experiment was carried out using the MIT Haystack radio antenna near Boston, and was named the Shapiro Effect after its discoverer, Professor Irwin Shapiro. We can safely say that a few microseconds either way will make no practical difference to our lives, although it may fascinate astrophysicists.

1: Time

> A RADIO SIGNAL BOUNCED OFF VENUS BACK TO EARTH HAS BEEN SHOWN TO BE SLOWED DOWN BY 200 MICROSECONDS OVER THE RETURN TRIP BECAUSE OF THE EFFECT OF PASSING THE HUGE MASS OF THE SUN.

Time is bitty

Cox was not happy with Einstein's view that all events exist already—it just doesn't feel right. It doesn't correlate with our own intuition and ignores quantum physics and the world of small particles where probabilities rule. He moves on finally to consider yet another view, this time from Professor Fay Dowker, a theoretical physicist at Imperial College.[16] She is trying to unify the smooth space-time continuum of Einstein with a belief that 'this material space-time fabric is itself fundamentally granular or "atomic".' This would 'enable physics to reclaim the notion of Becoming that seemed to have been lost with the advent of relativity'.

Cox concludes that the future is therefore not set in stone, but grows out of the past, which is more intuitive. He finally confesses that man cannot understand these things, but that we are asking questions. We need not belittle ourselves for failing to comprehend all the various theories about space and time. Scientists will always be puzzling over these things. The Bible is just as valid a source of information on origins, and arguably more so.

---

[16] http://www.imperial.ac.uk/people/f.dowker

1: Time

WE CAN TEST THE WORLD AROUND US AND
COSMIC SPACE TO SEE HOW IT REACTS TO
DIFFERENT EVENTS, AND FORMULATE LAWS OF
GRAVITATION AND THERMODYNAMICS, BUT WE
CAN NEVER TEST ORIGINS.

Understanding origins

There is a philosophical argument that man will never be able to arrive at the objective truth concerning the origin of the universe, together with the existence of time and space, unless a being standing apart from the space-time universe reveals it to him. No-one was around at the time of the creation, either of the universe or of man, to observe and record what happened. Furthermore, creation events are not capable of being subjected to the scientific method of hypothesis, experiment and observation, followed by refining that hypothesis into a theory. We can test the world around us and cosmic space to see how it reacts to different events, and formulate laws of gravitation and thermodynamics, but we can never test origins.

Maxwell was not only a great scientist; he also recognised the limitations of his science. He stated that 'Science is incompetent to reason upon the creation of matter itself out of nothing.' It is interesting that regarding the proposed theory of an evolving universe, he observed that a molecule of hydrogen in our brightest star system Sirius vibrates with the same frequency as it does on earth — it is exactly the same. On this basis he discounts an evolving universe: 'No theory of evolution can be formed to account for the similarity of molecules, for evolution necessarily implies continuous change, and the molecule is incapable of growth or decay, or generation or destruction.' [17]

---

[17] Lewis Campbell, and William Garnett, *op. cit.*, p359

More recently, we note the comments of the astronomer Professor Harry Van der Laan, who obtained his PhD at the Cavendish Laboratory, University of Cambridge, and later became Director General of the European Southern Observatory from 1988–1992. In 1966 he wrote that 'the origin of all things lies beyond our analytic grasp.' He argued that our scientific reasoning is limited to obtaining answers from 'increasingly precise analytic abstractions from the fulness of human experience... These ultimate questions which can be only haltingly, inadequately formulated, are religious questions, for the answers we accept determine the direction of our life. They can as such be adequately answered by the transcendent Word of the Creator.'[18]

---

[18] H. Van der Laan, *A Christian appreciation of physical science*, Christian Perspectives, The Association for Reformed Scientific Studies, Hamilton, Ontario, (1966), p19

Time and eternity in the Bible and Christian theology

The *Confessions* of Augustine
St. Augustine (A.D. 354–430) struggled to understand the nature of time and its relationship with eternity. He records his thoughts in the eleventh book of his *Confessions* (pp. 155–172). He saw how one's past history has gone for ever, apart from the shadows left by the memories recalled in the present time. The future has not yet come to pass, but one may see signs as to what is likely to occur. In his fourteenth book of *Confessions*, he argues 'But if the present were always present, and did not pass into past time, it obviously would not be time but eternity.'

'BUT IF THE PRESENT WERE ALWAYS PRESENT, AND DID NOT PASS INTO PAST TIME, IT OBVIOUSLY WOULD NOT BE TIME BUT ETERNITY.'

~ AUGUSTINE ~

He saw that eternity does not suffer the loss of the present or the absence of the future, but stands still in a steady state: 'Who will hold the heart of man that it may stand still and see how the eternity which always stands still is itself neither future nor past, but expresses itself in the times that are future and past?'

1: Time

He summed up his feelings on the matter in Book 22, confessing: 'My soul burns ardently to understand this most intricate enigma. O Lord ... to whom shall I confess my ignorance of these things with greater profit than to thee, to whom these studies of mine (ardently longing to understand thy Scriptures) are not a bore?' He thus acknowledged that the Scriptures are the only possible source of the revelation needed from outside our universe in order to begin to understand the realities which came into being with the creation of that same universe.

ST. AUGUSTINE STRUGGLED TO UNDERSTAND THE NATURE OF TIME AND ITS RELATIONSHIP WITH ETERNITY.

1: Time

Henry Vaughan

Henry Vaughan (1621–1695) was one of the metaphysical poets. He apparently sensed the very existence of eternity more strongly than most people, as he writes in *The World*:

THE WORLD

I saw Eternity the other night,
Like a great ring of pure and endless light,
All calm, as it was bright;
And round beneath it, Time in hours, days, years,
Driv'n by the spheres
Like a vast shadow mov'd; In which the world
And all her train were hurl'd …
But as I did their madness so discuss
One whisper'd thus,
'This ring the Bridegroom did for none provide,
But for his bride.'

The final two lines express his belief that Christ has reserved a future Eternity in light for those who belong to him, whom he loved and died for, his bride. In contrast, those belonging to the world, who only worshipped money and fame, like 'The fearful miser on a heap of rust', were doomed to be locked into a time-driven darkness.

1: Time

The twenty-first-century theologian Michael Reeves (President and Professor of Theology, Union School of Theology, Oxford) has summed up the natural man's view of eternity through the ages: 'What is it like in eternity? What is there? For millennia, the human imagination has groped and guessed, peering into the darkness. And in that darkness it has dreamed of dreadful gods and goddesses, of devils and powers, or of space and ultimate nothingness. Staggered by immensity, we are left terrified of what might be. If there is a God behind it all, what is he like?'[19]

WE ARE CREATURES OF TIME.

Time and eternity in the Bible

We will briefly look at what the Bible has to say on the subject of time and eternity, beginning with some quotes from Bible-believing Christians over the centuries. At the outset it has to be acknowledged that we are creatures of time. Everything we are and do incorporates a time factor. The very atoms within the organic molecules which compose our bodies vibrate at a certain frequency. Every sound we hear and image we view will be composed of wavelengths of the electromagnetic spectrum which oscillate at definite numbers of cycles per second (hertz). We are simply incapable of imagining what life in eternity, without the constraints of time, would be like. Nevertheless, we still want to push the boundaries of our knowledge as far as possible in trying to understand the concept of a timeless existence.

The Bible does not set out to satisfy our prying curiosity concerning the scientific description of the eternity of God's existence. Rather, it treats time as a gift from God which we have to value and use for God's glory and also our own enjoyment. Most think-

---

[19] Michael Reeves, *Christ Our Life*, Paternoster, Milton Keynes, 2014. ISBN 978-1-84227-758-4

ing Christians over the ages have majored on how we employ our time, but some, like Augustine, have also pondered on the eternal state. So we have to number our days and be ready to give an account as to how we have used this precious gift, for our answer will determine how we spend eternity—whether in the bliss of heaven, or in the anguish of hell. The best use of this gift of time is to seek to be reconciled to God through his precious Son Jesus Christ, who gave his life to rescue us from our dire predicament of death and transform us into his likeness so as to make us fit to live with him for all eternity in the joy of his presence. The worst use of time is to deliberately ignore God and all his sacrificial love for us. Let's see what some notable Christians have said on this topic.

THE BIBLE DOES NOT SET OUT TO SATISFY OUR PRYING CURIOSITY CONCERNING THE SCIENTIFIC DESCRIPTION OF THE ETERNITY OF GOD'S EXISTENCE. RATHER, IT TREATS TIME AS A GIFT FROM GOD WHICH WE HAVE TO VALUE AND USE FOR GOD'S GLORY AND ALSO OUR OWN ENJOYMENT.

1: Time

John Flavel

John Flavel (c.1627–1691) was a late Puritan minister and author. In his *Treatise of the Soul of Man* he wrote:

> Great is the worth and excellency of time, all the treasures of the world cannot protract, stop, or call back one minute of time. O what is man that the heavenly bodies should be wheeled about by Almighty Power in constant revolutions, to beget time for him! (Psalm 8:3).
>
> Invaluable are the things which God doth for men's souls in time. There are works wrought upon men's hearts in a seasonable hour in this life, which have an influence into the soul's happiness throughout eternity. There is a time of mercy, a time of love, viz. of illumination and conversion; and on that point of time, eternal life hangs in the whole weight of it.
>
> As soon as ever time shall end, eternity takes place. The stream of time delivers souls daily into the boundless ocean of vast eternity. We are now measured by time, hereafter by eternity.[20]

---

[20] John Flavel, *The Works of John Flavel*, Vol. 3, The Banner of Truth Trust, London, 1968, p15

John Tillotson

Dr. John Tillotson (1630–1694) was Archbishop of Canterbury from 1691–1694. He comments on the verse, 'But is now made manifest by the appearing of our Saviour Jesus Christ, who hath abolished death, and hath brought life and immortality to light through the gospel (2 Timothy 1:10 AV. Note: AV is the King James Authorised Version). 'Nothing can be more unbecoming Christians, whose whole religion pretends to be built upon the firm belief of another world, than to be intent upon the things of this present life, to the neglect of their souls and all eternity.'[21]

'NOTHING CAN BE MORE UNBECOMING CHRISTIANS ... THAN TO BE INTENT UPON THE THINGS OF THIS PRESENT LIFE, TO THE NEGLECT OF THEIR SOULS AND ALL ETERNITY.'

~ ARCHBISHOP JOHN TILLOTSON ~

---

[21] John Tillotson, *Sermons*, Vol. 9, Printed for C. Hitch et al., London, 1757, p385

1: Time

Matthew Henry

Matthew Henry (1662–1714), the famous Bible expositor, comments on verse 12 of Psalm 90: 'It is an excellent art rightly *to number our days,* so as not to be out in our calculation, as he was who counted upon many years to come when, that night, his soul was required of him.' On Luke 12 verse 21 he observes that 'It is the unspeakable folly of the most of men to mind and pursue the wealth of this world more than the wealth of the other world, that which is merely for the body and time, more than that which is for the soul and eternity.' [22]

'IT IS THE UNSPEAKABLE FOLLY OF THE MOST OF MEN TO MIND AND PURSUE THE WEALTH OF THIS WORLD MORE THAN THE WEALTH OF THE OTHER WORLD. . . '

~ MATTHEW HENRY ~

---

[22] Matthew Henry, *An Exposition of the Old and New Testament*, in 9 vols., James Nisbet & Co., London, 1866

Isaac Watts

Isaac Watts (1674–1748) was a preacher and hymnist, most remembered for such hymns as 'When I survey the wondrous cross' and 'O God our help in ages past'. He was also an author of essays or discourses, one of which, in the series on *The world to come*, was *The end of time*. He based his thoughts on a quote from John's Revelation: *And the angel which I saw stand upon the sea and upon the earth, lifted up his hand to heaven, and sware by him that liveth for ever and ever, … that there should be time no longer* (Revelation 10:5–6 AV). (Note: the ESV [English Standard Version] renders *time no longer* as *no more delay*.)

'DAYS AND MONTHS, AND YEARS, AND ALL THESE SHORT AND PAINFUL PERIODS OF TIME, SHALL BE SWALLOWED UP IN A LONG AND BLISSFUL ETERNITY.'

~ ISAAC WATTS ~

'Eternity comes upon us at once (suddenly), and all that we enjoy, all that we do, and all that we suffer in *Time, shall be no longer.*' He shows how there will be no more time for hoping to be better, or for mourning over wasted time, or for any chance of recovering

1: Time

lost time; we will have to give an account to God of our lives and eternal suffering will be the consequence of wasted time. 'Immortality is their dreadful portion … an immortality of sorrows.' He says that whereas the Christian will enjoy immortal life, the unbeliever will experience an awakened conscience with its eternal regrets.

Watts makes the appeal: 'Am I ready in all the powers of my nature, and made meet to enter into that unseen world, where there shall be no more of the revolutions of days and years, but one eternal day fills up all the space with divine pleasure, or one eternal night with long and deplorable distress and darkness?' He concludes that, for the Christian: 'Days and months, and years, and all these short and painful periods of time, shall be swallowed up in a long and blissful eternity … those felicities must be everlasting, for duration has no limit there, *time*, with all its measures, *shall be no more*. Amen.'[23]

'ETERNITY IS THAT WHICH CANNOT BE MADE LESS BY SUBTRACTION. IF WE TAKE FROM ETERNITY A THOUSAND YEARS OR AGES, THE REMAINDER IS NOT THE LESS FOR IT.'

~ JONATHAN EDWARDS ~

---

[23] Isaac Watts, , D.D., *The World to Come*, Evans & Bourne, London, 1814, pp3-27

Jonathan Edwards

Jonathan Edwards (1703–1758) was a leading figure in the American Great Awakening in the 1740s. In his graphic sermon *Natural Men in a Dreadful Condition* he writes: 'Eternity is that which cannot be made less by subtraction. If we take from eternity a thousand years or ages, the remainder is not the less for it. Eternity is that which will for ever be but beginning, and that because all the time which is past, let it be ever so long, is but a point to what remains. The wicked, after they have suffered millions of ages, will be, as it were, but in the first point, only setting out in their sufferings … The continuation of their torment cannot be measured out by revolutions of the sun, moon, or stars, by centuries or ages. They shall continue suffering after these heavens and this earth shall wax old as a garment, till the whole visible universe is dissolved.'

In contrast to the suffering of the wicked, Edwards describes the everlasting life enjoyed by the converted, and quotes from John's Gospel (4:14) — *The water that I shall give him shall be in him a well of water springing up into everlasting life:* 'This will make time comfortable, and will make the thoughts of eternity comfortable to you, when you shall have those pleasures which are at God's right hand for ever, in more immediate prospect; and shall have that faithful promise of God, that hereafter you shall see God, and shall dwell in his presence, and shall from the hands of Christ receive a crown of life.'[24]

---

[24] Jonathan Edwards, *A Narrative of Surprising Conversions*, Select Works of Jonathan Edwards, Vol. 1, The Banner of Truth Trust, London, 1965, pp181 & 203

1: Time

Hannah More

Hannah More (1745–1833) was a friend of William Wilberforce (1759–1833) the abolitionist. She was a Christian educator, writer and social reformer. She ends her essay *On Time, Considered as a Talent* thus: 'He who cannot find time to consult his Bible, will find one day, that he has time to be sick; he who has no time to pray, must find time to die. He who can find no time to reflect, is most likely to find time to sin; he who cannot find time for repentance, will find an eternity in which repentance will be of no avail ... Is it not obvious, then, that the design of life is to prepare for judgment; and that in proportion as we employ time well, we make immortality happy?'[25]

Commemorative stamp featuring Hannah More

---

[25] Hannah More, *The Works of Hannah More*, Vol. 9 of 11, T. Cadell, London, 1830, p136

James Henley Thornwell

James Henley Thornwell (1812–1862) was an American Presbyterian pastor and a professor at South Carolina College. While on a voyage to Europe in 1841 to improve his failing health, he wrote to his wife some observations on his fellow-passengers. 'I was much struck with the various efforts of my fellow-passengers to while away the time. Though they would have shuddered at the thought of death, they evidently had more time than they knew what to do with. They tried cards, and dice, and chess; they would walk, and yawn, and smoke, and loll; and after all, sigh out in awful moans under the intolerable burden of too much time. Ah me! On a dying bed these wasted hours will be like fiends from hell, to torture and harass the burdened soul. How important is the caution of the Apostle, "Redeeming the time!" Mark that word, redeeming. It implies scarcity; it teaches that time must be *purchased*; but who, until a dying hour, now finds time scarce, or feels constrained to buy it?'[26]

---

[26] B. M. Palmer, *The Life and Letters of James Henley Thornwell*, The Banner of Truth Trust, Edinburgh, 1986 (reprint), p162

1: Time

Louis Berkhof

Louis Berkhof (1873–1957) was a Dutch-American theologian who became President of Calvin Theological Seminary and is remembered for his major work *Systematic Theology* in which he writes concerning the verse 'In the beginning God created the heavens and the earth' (Genesis 1:1): 'It would seem best to take the expression in the absolute sense as an indication of the beginning of all temporal things and even of time itself ... Technically speaking, it is not correct to assume that time was already in existence when God created the world, and that He in some point in that existing time, called 'the beginning' brought forth the universe. Time is only one of the forms of all created existence, and therefore could not exist before creation. For that reason, Augustine thought it would be more correct to say that the world was created *cum tempore* (with time) than to assert that it was created *in tempore* (in time).'[27]

'TIME IS ONLY ONE OF THE FORMS OF ALL CREATED EXISTENCE, AND THEREFORE COULD NOT EXIST BEFORE CREATION.'

~ LOUIS BERKHOF ~

---

[27] Louis Berkhof, *Systematic Theology*, The Banner of Truth Trust, London, 1966 (reprint), p130

Aiden Wilson Tozer

Aiden Wilson Tozer (1897–1963) was an American pastor and noted Christian author. He advocated holy, spiritual living and the need to know God better. In his *The Knowledge of the Holy*, he observed with Berkhof that 'Time marks the beginning of created existence, and because God never began to exist it can have no application to Him.' Tozer adds, 'Because God lives in an everlasting now, He has no past and no future. When time-words occur in the Scriptures they refer to our time, not to His … God dwells in eternity but time dwells in God. He's already lived all our tomorrows as He's lived all our yesterdays.'[28] God knows perfectly what is to come, nothing can take him by surprise, and he is sovereignly in control. This leads to the concept that as far as God is concerned, all of the past, the present, and the future, is condensed into an eternal present.

'BECAUSE GOD LIVES IN AN EVERLASTING NOW,
HE HAS NO PAST AND NO FUTURE.'

~ A. W. TOZER ~

---

[28] Aiden Wilson Tozer, *The Knowledge of the Holy*, Chapter 7, *The Eternity of God*, Authentic, Milton Keynes, 2010 (reprint), p51

1: Time

D. Martyn Lloyd-Jones

Dr. D. Martyn Lloyd-Jones (1899–1981) was the most famous British preacher of the twentieth century. Born in Cardiff, Wales, his family later moved to London, where he qualified in medicine at St. Bartholomew's Hospital. He was a brilliant student, soon becoming a heart specialist and assistant to Lord Horder, the Royal Physician. He was called to the ministry, pastoring a church in South Wales at Aberavon for ten years, then returning to London to minister at Westminster Chapel. His long series of sermons on the book of *Romans* have been published as 14 volumes by the Banner of Truth. The following quote is from the volume on *Romans* chapter 8:17–39, *The Final Perseverance of the Saints*, and comes from Chapter 3, which deals with verse 18 (AV): 'For I reckon that the sufferings of this present time are not worthy to be compared with the glory which shall be revealed in us.'

'ETERNITY! WHEN YOU THINK OF IT, WHAT IS THIS LIFE OF OURS … IT IS JUST LIKE A BREATH, AN EXHALATION. IT IS NOTHING IN COMPARISON WITH ETERNITY.'

~ D. MARTYN LLOYD-JONES ~

1: Time

Time! What a burden time is when you are looking forward to something! How it seems to drag! If you are not a Christian you have to answer that problem; you have just to resign yourself to your fate, and 'go on with it'. But that is not how the Christian looks at time. The Christian has a view which enables him to handle time as it ought to be handled. He says, 'Yes, here I am in this world. I may have to live another ten, twenty, thirty, forty, fifty, sixty, even seventy years. I look at it as a man, and in earthly terms, and it seems a terribly long time. But when I think of eternity, when I think of the glory that is coming in eternity, everything changes.' Eternity! There is no end to it! Can you think of a million years? Well, multiply that by a million, and multiply that by a million, and go on and on for ever and ever, and there is still no end. Eternity! When you think of it, what is this life of ours … It is just like a breath, an exhalation. It is nothing in comparison with eternity.[29]

A Practical View
Lloyd-Jones, known as 'the Doctor', has come to this verse which is looking at Christians who are enduring suffering of various types. Sometimes, in the case of martyrdom, as the Apostle Paul was to undergo, there is no medicine which can alleviate the pain of the inevitable death. There was, however, the hope of eternal joy to comfort them in their predicament. We may take a philosophical view of the subject of time and eternity, and indeed, find it fascinating. Here in this passage, however, is a practical view of the same subjects, which will support all believers as they approach their own deaths.

---

[29] D. Martyn Lloyd-Jones, *Romans—Exposition of Chapter 8:17-39*, The Final Perseverance of the Saints, The Banner of Truth Trust, Edinburgh, 1987 (reprint), p40

Edward (Ted) Donnelly

Ted Donnelly is New Testament Professor Emeritus at Reformed Theological College, Belfast. In his popular book *Heaven and Hell*, he writes concerning the instinctive longing for eternity which is found in everyone:

> Praise God for heaven! For every good longing within us is an intimation of immortality, an echo of eternity in our souls, a pointer to everlasting life. We were not created for seventy short years, 'not born for death', in the poet's words. Our Creator did not design beings of such complexity and capacity for a mere handful of decades. 'He has put eternity in their hearts' (Ecclesiastes 3:11) and we have not been redeemed to be frustrated … God has an eternity planned for us to blossom in.[30]

---

[30] Edward Donnelly, *Heaven and Hell*, The Banner of Truth Trust, Edinburgh, 2001, p125

Time in the Bible

God's eternity

The Bible teaches that God is eternal; he is timeless and unaffected by time. God dwells in eternity: 'The eternal God is your dwelling place' (Deuteronomy 33:27). Not only that, he created time and created the universe and mankind to be regulated and bound by the constraints of time. God remains sovereign over time, and can change such things as the day-length or orbits of the planets if he so wishes. Living in time was a most pleasurable thing until sin, followed by disease, death and decay, entered the world as an inevitable consequence following man's rebellion against his Maker.

> GOD REMAINS SOVEREIGN OVER TIME, AND CAN CHANGE SUCH THINGS AS THE DAY-LENGTH OR ORBITS OF THE PLANETS IF HE SO WISHES.

We saw how Tozer believed that God dwells in an everlasting now, comprising past, present and future, over all of which God is sovereign. The Scriptures give us hints of the nature of God's eternity. When Moses asked God his name, God replied, 'I am who I am' (Exodus 3:14). This is a God who is the always present 'I am'. In the Revelation of the apostle John, God again declares his eternal existence as follows, '"I am the Alpha and the Omega," says the Lord God, "who is and who was and who is to come, the Almighty"' (Rev. 1:8). Jesus himself claims the same title in Rev. 22:13, 'I am the Alpha and the Omega, the first and the last, the beginning and the end,' and so declares he is of the same divine essence as the Father. God doesn't change with changing circumstances, but sees all of history, together with the present and future, in an instant.

Is eternity simply time which never ends, or is it the absence of time? We cannot know for certain, but perhaps it will reflect the continuous present in which God dwells, and incorporates all past

1: Time

earthly events and future heavenly events. This will only be fully understood when we have our resurrected bodies (1 Corinthians 15:44), which Paul looks forward to when he comments: 'Now I know in part; then I shall know fully, even as I have been fully known' (1 Cor. 13:12b).

T. S. Eliot

It is interesting that, as the poet T. S. Eliot (1888–1965), in his *Four Quartets—1. Burnt Norton*, grappled with the idea of time, his natural reason led to a conclusion concerning the nature of eternity which is probably not so far from the truth:

> *Time present and time past*
> *Are both perhaps present in time future,*
> *And time future contained in time past.*
> *If all time is eternally present*
> *All time is unredeemable ...*
> *Time past and time future*
> *What might have been and what has been*
> *Point to one end, which is always present.*

T. S. Eliot described himself as having 'a Catholic cast of mind, a Calvinist heritage, and a Puritanical temperament'. He converted from Unitarianism to become an Anglo-Catholic in 1927, and published the Four Quartets between 1936–1942, for which he was awarded the Nobel Prize in Literature in 1948.

William Lane Craig

William Lane Craig (born 1949), the American Christian apologist, has made a detailed study of God's relationship with time and eternity. He concludes: 'God exists timelessly without creation and temporally subsequent to creation.'[31]

Man's mortality
In contrast to God's eternity, we are entirely locked into time. Time machines are wholly fictional, so can provide no escape route. The beating of our hearts and the nervous impulses in our brains are time-bound events which define our existence.

At death or at the Second Coming, we must all cross over from the world of time into the eternal world. But how can we do this, and where can we get the power to obtain this eternal existence? God's eternity is an essential part of his very being. Another characteristic he possesses is omnipotence. God, therefore, has the power to be able to give eternal life to his adopted children: 'The gift of God is eternal life in Christ Jesus our Lord' (Romans 6:23). The apostle John records Jesus' words to Nicodemus: 'For God so loved the world, that he gave his only Son, that whoever believes in him should not perish but have eternal life' (John 3:16).

Jesus was saying that if anyone trusts him completely as Lord, repents of sin, believes his words when he says he is the Son of God and has come to die for their sins, and seeks to obey his commandments, then all such people will receive the unearned gift of immortal life and go to heaven when they die.

---

[31] http://www.reasonablefaith.org/god-time-and-eternity#ixzz3XS8prb8j

1: Time

Everlasting life
Christ offers us eternal and everlasting life in contrast to perishing (John 3:16). The immediate context of a word is vital to its interpretation, as also its wider context in comparison with other Scriptures. The context here is a contrast between perishing and having everlasting life. Although it does not say 'everlasting perishing', that could be inferred from the immediate context and confirmed from our Lord's own words on the subject. Even in this famous Gospel text, there is a balance between speaking of both heaven and hell. Other texts show that all people have immortal souls which, following death, will either experience torment or the blessings of immortal life with Christ in heaven.[32]

Valuing time
The Bible also has instructions connected with our responsible use of time. As More and Thornwell observed above, we must employ our time well and make every moment count by 'making best use of (redeeming) the time, because the days are evil' (Eph. 5:16, my parenthesis). Psalm 90, written by Moses, is all about the role time plays in our lives and how God is in control of our destinies.

'The days of our lives are seventy, or even by virtue of strength eighty' (v. 10a). Moses goes on to ask God to 'teach us to number our days that we may get a heart of wisdom' (v. 12). Verse 5 of this Psalm has been immortalised by Isaac Watts (1674–1748) in his hymn *Our God, our help in ages past*:

> *Time, like an ever-rolling stream,*
> *Bears all its sons away;*
> *They fly forgotten, as a dream*
> *Dies at the opening day.*

---

[32] Nigel T. Faithfull, *A Lost Eternity?*, Reformation Today, 254, Jul-Aug 2013, 2-5; and Nigel T. Faithfull, *'Tis Immortality*, Reformation Today, 255, Sept-Oct 2013, 5-8.

1: Time

Being ready

The New Testament points us to the future-coming of the Lord Jesus Christ to claim his bride, the church, and to judge the world. In the light of this, we are all urged to seek an 'out of court settlement' with God before it is too late.

The first message Jesus declared in his earthly ministry was, 'The time is fulfilled, and the kingdom of God is at hand. Repent and believe in the gospel' (Mark 1:15). Jesus later told us, 'Therefore you also must be ready, for the Son of Man is coming at an hour you do not expect' (Matthew 24:44). Peter, in his older and wiser years, exhorts believers, 'The end of all things is at hand, therefore be self-controlled and sober-minded for the sake of your prayers' (1 Peter 4:7).

Our perception of time

Thornwell observed how his fellow passengers on the ship moaned 'under the intolerable burden of too much time.' How do we perceive the passing of time? Our view of time is that it is real, and has been created by the God, who also sovereignly controls the course of history. Our knowledge, however, is limited, which means we will always have a subjective element to our understanding of time.

John Calvin

'WHEN WE LIFT OUR HEARTS HEAVENWARDS, A THOUSAND YEARS BEGINS TO BE LIKE A MOMENT.'

~ JOHN CALVIN ~

1: Time

We are all aware on occasions of time 'dragging' by so slowly, and yet 'flying by' when we are enjoying ourselves. Time, however, is not merely subjective; it is a wonderful gift of God. John Calvin (1509–1564) noted the subjective appearance of time when he said, 'If we look around us, a moment can seem a long time, but when we lift our hearts heavenwards, a thousand years begins to be like a moment.'[33] He also commented on 2 Peter 3:8: 'For waiting seems very long on this account, because we have our eyes fixed on the shortness of the present life, and we also increase weariness by computing days, hours, and minutes. But when the eternity of God's kingdom comes to our minds, many ages vanish away like so many moments … do ye then ascend in your minds to heaven, and thus time will be to you neither long nor short.'

How do we perceive the passing of time? Our view of time is that it is real, and has been created by the God, who also sovereignly controls the course of history.

---

[33] Quoted by John Blanchard, *The Complete Gathered Gold*, Evangelical Press, Darlington, 2007 (reprint), p636

The End

The universe as we presently perceive it will one day come to an end, and will be replaced by a new heaven and a new earth (Revelation 21:1). Considering John's Gospel, chapter 12, verses 44–50, Bishop J. C. Ryle (1816–1900) solemnly observes:

> There is a last day! The world shall not always go on as it does now. Buying and selling, sowing and reaping, planting and building, marrying and giving in marriage,—all this shall come to an end at last. There is a time appointed by the Father when the whole machinery of creation shall stop, and the present dispensation shall be changed for another. It had a beginning, and it shall also have an end. Banks shall at length close their doors for ever. Stock exchanges shall be shut. Parliaments shall be dissolved. The very sun, which since Noah's flood has done his daily work so faithfully, shall rise and set no more. Well would it be if we thought more of this day! Rent-days, birth-days, wedding-days, are often regarded as days of absorbing interest; but they are nothing compared to the last day. There is a judgment coming! Men have their reckoning days, and God will at last have His. The trumpet shall sound. The dead shall be raised incorruptible. The living shall be changed. All, of every name and nation, and people and tongue, shall

1: Time

stand before the judgment seat of Christ. The books shall be opened, and the evidence brought forth. Our true character will come out before the world. There will be no concealment, no evasion, no false colouring. Every one shall give account of himself to God, and all shall be judged according to their works. The wicked shall go away into everlasting fire, and the righteous into life eternal.[34]

'MEN HAVE THEIR RECKONING DAYS, AND
GOD WILL AT LAST HAVE HIS.'

~ J. C. RYLE ~

Our last opportunity
We began by looking at time in a rather detached philosophical or scientific way. We have ended by seeing how the Bible makes the subject of time a very personal matter. Whether we believe the Bible or not, we have to decide for ourselves how we are going to spend our lives. Are we going to seek to help our fellow human beings, or are we going to be utterly selfish, and follow what amounts to a 'survival of the fittest' philosophy? The Bible adds

---

[34] J. C Ryle, *Expository Thoughts On John* - John 12:44-50, Robert Carter and Bros., New York, 1878, pp372-373; available at:
https://ia902708.us.archive.org/18/items/expositorythough06ryle/expositorythough06ryle.pdf

another dimension to consider: how are we going to spend the time God has entrusted us with and, in particular, how are we going to relate to a God who is altogether pure and holy? Some clues have already been given as to what is required.

The ending of the time in which we now live will therefore also mean the ending of the opportunity God has given all people to repent of their sin and unbelief, to turn to him and accept the forgiveness and righteousness which, by his grace, he freely offers to us.

Whatever our views of time and eternity, God has left us in no doubt that the 'now' we experience each day is a moment of opportunity which can never be repeated. That is why Paul exhorts us, 'Behold, now is the favourable time; behold, now is the day of salvation' (2 Corinthians 6:2). The frightening thing is that those who refuse to accept God's cleansing will be locked into their dirty condition for all eternity, whereas those who have confessed their sin to God will be kept safe and clean for ever (1 John 1:9; Revelation 22:11). As the saying goes, 'where the tree falls, there it will lie' (Ecclesiastes 11:3b).

How will you spend eternity? Are you ready to welcome the return of the Lord Jesus Christ, like Josiah Conder (1789–1855) in his hymn 'See the ransomed millions stand'?

Time has nearly reached its sum;
All things, with Thy bride, say 'Come!'
Jesus, whom all worlds adore,
Come and reign for evermore!

2

SPACE

*Great are the works of the Lord,
studied by all who delight in them.*

Psalm 111:2

Out there

In the chapter on Time we were surfing around the universe on the curves of Einstein's space-time continuum. Imagine we have ended up on the remotest galaxy from planet Earth, and now it is time to return home. We will travel at the fastest possible speed—the speed of light.[1]

Astronomers in the USA have estimated that light from the farthest known galaxy has taken 13.1 billion years to reach Earth. We would not even live long enough to exit that galaxy, let alone reach our own planet.

Andromeda

There are about 200 billion galaxies in the observable universe. The nearest galaxy to our own is the spiral galaxy Andromeda. It has a trillion (10^{12}) stars and is 2.5 million light years from Earth. Bearing in mind that light travels at about 671 million miles per hour, in one year it will have gone 23,397,960 million miles. That is in just one year; but supposing we work out how far light would travel in 2.5 million years, we get the (literally) astronomical figure of about 15,000,000,000,000,000,000 miles. That is a long, long way away! We should be beginning to see just how vast is the space occupied by our universe.

The Milky Way

Our own galaxy is the called the Milky Way. It is shaped like a disc, but because we are looking out from inside it, the appearance is of a milky white band across the night sky. It may be comprised of about 400 billion stars, but the truth is that they are too difficult to count, so an approximation of their number is made by estimating the mass of the galaxy, and then correlating that to the average number of stars expected in such a mass. The diameter of the galaxy is about 100,000 light years (5.88×10^{17} miles).

Our Sun is just one out of the 400 billion stars, and forms the

---

[1] http://physicsworld.com/cws/article/news/2013/oct/23/farthest-confirmed-galaxy-is-a-prolific-star-creator

centre of our Solar System. The Sun has a diameter of 109 times that of the Earth, which orbits around it at a distance of about 93 million miles. There are seven other major planets: Mercury is nearest the Sun, followed by Venus, Earth, Mars, Jupiter, Saturn, Uranus and Neptune. There are also dwarf planets like Pluto, and minor planets, moons and comets.

> WE ON PLANET EARTH ARE LIVING ON THE THIRD PLANET FROM THE SUN. IT IS UNIQUELY POSITIONED SO THAT IT IS NEITHER TOO HOT NOR TOO COLD FOR LIFE TO BE SUSTAINED.

The Goldilocks Zone
Distances from the Sun are measured in terms of Astronomical Units (AU), where 1 AU is about 93 million miles, corresponding to the distance of Earth from the Sun. Mercury lies at 0.4 AU and Neptune at 30.1 AU. We on planet Earth are living on the third planet from the Sun. It is uniquely positioned so that it is neither too hot nor too cold for life to be sustained. As mentioned earlier, we are living in what has been termed the Goldilocks Zone, where the temperature is 'just right'. This habitable zone can only exist within narrow limits of about from 0.99 to 1.7 AU. Any nearer to the Sun, and the Earth's surface water would boil away. This effect is somewhat mitigated by air circulation patterns called Hadley Cells which operate between the equator and the poles. Recent research using computer modelling allows Earth to be habitable as close as 0.95 AU from the Sun, but it is still a relatively narrow region.[2]

---

[2] Jérémy Leconte et al., Increased insolation threshold for runaway greenhouse processes on Earth-like planets, Nature, Dec. 11, 2013

Crescent Earth: View from the Moon

The tilt—our seasons

The Earth rotates around the Sun once every year. Its axis is now tilted at an angle of 23.44 degrees. In fact, it oscillates between 22.1 and 24.5 degrees over a 41,000 year cycle. This tilt is the cause of our seasons. It is summer in the northern hemisphere when the North Pole is tilted towards the Sun, and winter when tilted away from the Sun. Spring and autumn occur at the intermediate positions.

The spin—our days
The Earth spins around its axis in an anti-clockwise direction as viewed from the North Star. The solar day length consists of 3600x24 = 86,400 solar seconds. The length of these seconds fluctuates randomly by about 5 milliseconds due to core-mantle coupling. Tidal friction has also caused the mean solar day to be longer by up to 2 milliseconds than in 1972, when the leap second was introduced to compensate.

The moon—our lunar months
The moon is a quarter of the diameter of the Earth which it orbits in an ellipse at a mean distance of 238,857 miles once every 27.3 days. Its gravitational attraction is a cause of the tides in the sea. It is the largest planetary satellite relative to the size of the planet it orbits.

Is there a purpose?
We have seen some of the facts about where we find ourselves in this immense but wonderful universe. These details on their own, however, hardly give our lives the meaning and purpose we are seeking. What sense can we make of it all? Scientific humanists would say that we are here merely because the conditions which make life sustainable happen by chance to exist on the Earth. The many factors which all need to be present at the same time, no matter how improbable, exist on Earth—temperature, water, a perfect blend of gases with oxygen in the atmosphere, a suitable day length and restful dark periods allowing refreshing and re-energising sleep. No other similar planet has yet been discovered; scientists just keep repeating that, because so many galaxies with trillions of heavenly bodies exist, there must be other planets like ours somewhere out there. Even if there was another planet a bit like ours, that would still not give us a reason for being here or a purpose for life.

Life without purpose

Life without an ultimate purpose becomes unbearable. When the end of such a purposeless life is approaching, a life where celebrating the pleasure of our senses was all that delighted us, then the dark meaningless future which looms ahead of us becomes too much to bear. It makes the sensitive soul want to rage against the loss of everything that had mattered. Dylan Thomas (1914–1953) exclaimed:

> *Do not go gentle into that good night,*
> *Old age should burn and rave at close of day;*
> *Rage, rage against the dying of the light.*

ALBERT CAMUS WAS FACED WITH A DUALISM WHICH WAS IMPOSSIBLE TO RESOLVE. AND WHICH LED TO HIS SUPPORT FOR THE PHILOSOPHY OF THE ABSURD.

Albert Camus

Thomas's contemporary, the French atheist philosopher and Nobel Laureate, Albert Camus (1913–1960), was aware from his enjoyment of playing football that there was certainly meaning in mutual support and teamwork, but this contradicted his atheistic philosophy that left him in a meaningless universe. He was faced with a dualism which was impossible to resolve. It led to his support for the philosophy of the absurd. He said, 'If nothing had any meaning, you would be right. But there is something that still has a meaning.'[3]

---

[3] Albert Camus, from Second *Letter to a German Friend*, (originally written in December, 1943), in *Resistance, Rebellion and Death*, Vintage Books, 1988, p. 14

He explains further:

> I continue to believe that this world has no ultimate meaning. But I know that something in it has a meaning and that is man, because he is the only creature to insist on having one. This world has at least the truth of man, and our task is to provide its justifications against fate itself. And it has no justification but man; hence he must be saved if we want to save the idea we have of life. With your scornful smile you will ask me: what do you mean by saving man? And with all my being I shout to you that I mean not mutilating him and yet giving a chance to the justice that man alone can conceive.[4]

Man's best philosophy

The best that man can come up with is that without God's revelation, we are living in a meaningless universe, yet we know there has to be meaning in mutual love and sympathy, beauty and art, and the scientific marvels of law and order in the universe. Many people just live out their lives, trying to enjoy themselves and being helpful to others, but without any sure hope for the future. They try to bring meaning into their little worlds without worrying themselves over the issues which troubled Camus, but life could be so much richer and more comforting if there was indeed a meaning and purpose to everything, and if one could be certain there was a life after death.

> CHRISTIANS WOULD SAY THAT GOD HAD A PLAN WHEN HE FIRST MADE THE IDEAL ENVIRONMENT FOR LIVING BEINGS, AND THEN CREATED PEOPLE TO INHABIT IT.

---

[4] Albert Camus, Fourth *Letter to a German Friend*, (originally written in 1944), in *Resistance, Rebellion and Death*, Vintage Books, 1988, p. 28

The Christian viewpoint

The Christian would reverse the argument of the scientific humanist or atheist. We would say that God had a plan when he first made the ideal environment for living beings, and then created people to inhabit it. The apostle Paul tells us that God '... who saved us and called us to a holy calling, not because of our works but *because of his own purpose* and grace, which he gave us in Christ Jesus *before the ages began*, and which now has been manifested through the appearing of our Saviour Christ Jesus, who abolished death and brought life and immortality to light through the gospel ...' (2 Timothy 1:9–10, italics added). God had a purpose in mind before the creation and before time and 'the ages' began.

God gives space to humanity

After God had made the first people, Adam and Eve, he gave them a purpose and brought a structure into their lives. Firstly we read, 'And God blessed them. And God said to them, "Be fruitful and multiply and fill the earth and subdue it, and have dominion over the fish of the sea and over the birds of the heavens and over every living thing that moves on the earth"' (Genesis 1:28). They had been presented with the grand destiny of extending their families with permission to spread out over all the earth, and to manage and conserve all the creatures that God had made. They had as much space as they needed and could live wherever they liked. Man's duty to bring God's rule over all his creation is known as the cultural mandate—a specific command of God which gives an overall purpose to life. This is to be done in fellowship and communion with God. Adam and Eve could converse directly with God to start with, and we now have the Bible to get guidance regarding our moral duties and responsibilities.

Secondly, God made man with a psyche and constitution which gains satisfaction and becomes healthy through suitable work. 'The LORD God took the man and put him in the garden of Eden to work it and keep it' (Genesis 2:15). There is a dignity to work and labour, whatever form it takes, and whether as self-employed or employed by someone else, or doing domestic and family duties at home.

Thirdly, Adam was given the task of naming the animals, which we now call taxonomy. 'Now out of the ground the LORD God had formed every beast of the field and every bird of the heavens and brought them to the man to see what he would call them. And whatever the man called the living creature, that was its name' (Genesis 2:19).

A helper for Adam

At the same time as Adam was engaged in this task, he was evaluating whether any of the creatures fulfilled his basic needs of companionship and support in this work—but none came up to the mark. The following verses tell us how God put Adam into a deep sleep and, apparently making an incision, took one of his ribs and closed the flesh up again. From this rib, a part of Adam, God made his wife Eve (Genesis 2:21–25). The Bible expositor, Matthew Henry (1662–1714), comments: 'That the woman was *made of a rib out of the side of Adam;* not made out of his head to rule over him, nor out of his feet to be trampled upon by him, but out of his side to be equal with him, under his arm to be protected, and near his heart to be beloved.'[5] The Bible insists that although women may have different roles from men in certain situations, they have equal created dignity and deserve the same respect as men.

---

[5] Quoted in Nigel Faithfull, *Thoughts Fixed and Affections Flaming*, Day One, 2012, p45

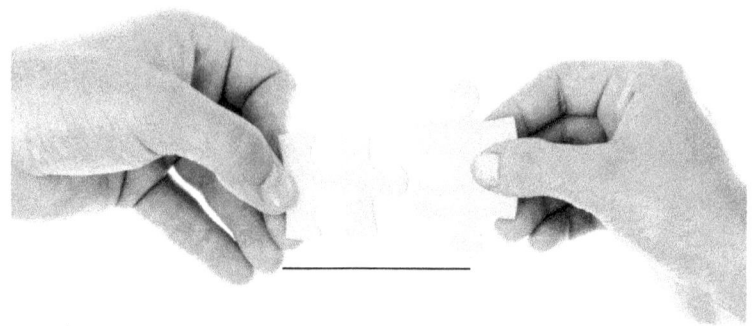

'THE WOMAN WAS MADE OF A RIB OUT OF THE SIDE OF ADAM; NOT MADE OUT OF HIS HEAD TO RULE OVER HIM, NOR OUT OF HIS FEET TO BE TRAMPLED UPON BY HIM, BUT OUT OF HIS SIDE TO BE EQUAL WITH HIM, UNDER HIS ARM TO BE PROTECTED, AND NEAR HIS HEART TO BE BELOVED.'

~ MATTHEW HENRY ~

God orders time and the working week

God knew that men and women would not keep healthy in body and soul if they worked 24:7. It had been intended that they would find satisfaction in work, but they had not been designed to work incessantly. There needed to be a structure to time, and for periods of work to be interspersed with times set apart for rest and relaxation, and for worship and meditation. The soul needed feeding as well as the body.

God therefore did two things. He firstly organised the sun, moon and stars to give light at the appropriate times, and caused the tilt of the Earth to introduce the seasons.

'And God said, "Let there be lights in the expanse of the heavens to separate the day from the night. And let them be for signs and for seasons, and for days and years ..."' (Genesis 1:14).

GOD HIMSELF FOUND SATISFACTION IN TAKING
TIME TO REFLECT ON EVERYTHING THAT
HE HAD CREATED.

God gives us a day for rest

God himself found satisfaction in taking time to reflect on everything that he had created:

'And on the seventh day God finished the work that he had done, and he rested on the seventh day from all his work that he had done. So God blessed the seventh day and made it holy, because on it God rested from all his work that he had done in creation' (Genesis 2:2–3). God had proposed earlier: 'Let us make man in our image, after our likeness' (Genesis 1:26a), and so we also were intended to follow God's pattern of resting on one day in seven. Moses, under God's command, enshrined this creation principle in the fourth commandment:

'Remember the Sabbath day, to keep it holy. Six days you shall labour, and do all your work, but the seventh day is a Sabbath to the LORD your God. On it you shall not do any work, you, or your son, or your daughter, your male servant, or your female servant, or your livestock, or the sojourner who is within your gates. For in six days the LORD made heaven and earth, the sea, and all that is in them, and rested on the seventh day. Therefore the LORD blessed the Sabbath day and made it holy' (Exodus 20:8–11).

French Republican Calendar

On October 23, 1793, just nine days after Queen Marie-Antoinette was executed, the Republican Calendar was decreed. This was an attempt to de-Christianise the Gregorian calendar with its associations with Roman Catholicism and Christianity, which were considered as superstitions. Reason was in, and religion was out. The new calendar was considered scientific and each month was divided into three 'weeks' of ten days followed by a day of rest. The chief architect of the calendar, Charles-Gilbert Romme (1750–1795), said that its chief object was to abolish Sunday. The Republican Calendar was finally abolished by Napoleon a little over twelve years after it was legislated, and France returned to the Gregorian calendar on January 1, 1806.[6]

Stalin's six-day week

In Stalinist Soviet Russia, experiments were made with a five-day week and, in the 1930s, a six-day week. Employees would work five days, then take a day off and return to work the next day. Family members would often have different shift patterns, so would not share the same day's rest. It was an attempt to maintain continuous working in the factories and so increase productivity, but was also part of an attempt to eliminate religion. Following a decree dated 26 June 1940, the traditional interrupted seven-day week with Sunday as the common day of rest was reintroduced on 27 June 1940.[7]

Both these attempts to tinker with God's plan for the structure of time and its division into suitable periods of work and rest were found to be unworkable and unsustainable. Even the factory machines could not keep working 24:7 and needed periods for regular maintenance. Our lives will always profit from having a due regard to the laws which God has woven into the fabric of the universe.

---

[6] https://www.worldslastchance.com/ecourses/lessons/changing-weeks-hiding-sabbath-ecourse/18/french-republican-calendar.html

[7] https://en.wikipedia.org/wiki/Soviet_calendar

Noah's Flood and the seasons

Global warming

At the present time there is great international concern over the effects of global warming. Developing economies are increasing industrial output to boost their economies, but that inevitably means that they will increase their carbon dioxide output. This gas traps the sun's energy, giving the greenhouse effect, which causes the ambient temperature to rise. Trees will absorb carbon dioxide, converting it into the cellulose (50%), hemicellulose (30%) and lignin (20%) which make up the dry material of the wood (typical figures). In exchange, the trees release life-giving oxygen back into the atmosphere.[8]

CARBON DIOXIDE TRAPS THE SUN'S ENERGY, GIVING THE GREENHOUSE EFFECT, WHICH CAUSES THE AMBIENT TEMPERATURE TO RISE.

Unfortunately, deforestation of the rain forests by human activity has reduced the total surface area covered by such forests on our planet from 15% to 6%. This is hardly a wise way of exercising man's God-given dominion over the environment.[9]

Whatever the arguments which abound on the real or apparent effects of global warming, there will always be a need for good forest management, and a programme for replacing trees that are felled. Until such time as the rising carbon dioxide content of the atmosphere has been attenuated, however, our summers could become unbearably hot, and the ice-caps could be in danger of

---

[8] http://www.learn.forestbioenergy.net/learning-modules/module-6/unit-1/lesson-1
[9] https://ypte.org.uk/factsheets/rainforests/what-are-the-threats-to-the-rainforests

2: Space

further melting to cause widespread flooding. We might also miss seeing snow in winter until the atmospheric quality has been restored. Bearing this in mind, we should not live in fear that the seasons we love and have grown up with are in danger of being permanently lost. Although parts of the world experience harsh localised droughts and environmental disasters, the Bible assures us such a catastrophe in our climate will never occur again on the global scale which occurred in the days of Noah, and which we will next briefly mention.

The Flood

Tales of an ancient flood occur in the cultural records of many ancient empires, such as the Mesopotamian, Hindu texts from India, the story of Deucalion who built an ark to survive a flood in Greek mythology, and Bergelmir the fabled Norse frost giant who survived a flood of blood by climbing on a floating object. The Mayans in South America and Native Americans in North America also had ancient flood stories. The biblical text of Genesis (chapters 6 to 8) gives a full account of the incident which featured Noah and his family.

After about 1,500 years from the time of the creation, the people on the Earth had multiplied, but man had become so very wicked and violent that 'every intention of the thoughts of his heart was only evil continually' (Genesis 6:5b). God thought to destroy both man and beast from the Earth, but Noah was different and found grace in God's eyes. God therefore warned Noah of the coming flood, and gave him precise instructions on how to build a large floating barge, the Ark, in which anyone who wished could be saved. In the end, the people presumably thought the whole scheme was foolish, and only Noah's family was saved. The apostle Peter records that the people suffered: 'because they formerly did not obey, when God's patience waited in the days of Noah, while the ark was being prepared, in which a few, that is, eight persons, were brought safely through water' (1 Peter 3:20). Again, Jesus himself said: 'They were eating and drinking and marrying and being given in marriage, until the day when Noah entered the ark and the flood came and destroyed them all' (Luke 17:27).

Apart from the authority of God's word, there is the worldwide evidence of fossil-bearing sedimentary strata which is strong evidence that a large flood must have occurred. The effects of more localised tsunamis and melting glaciers at the end of an ice age must also be taken into account in assessing the data.

Stability of the seasons

We have been considering the Flood because of a promise God made to Noah just after he had emerged from the Ark after the Flood and offered burnt offerings on the altar he had made. God promised, 'While the earth remains, seedtime and harvest, cold and heat, summer and winter, day and night, shall not cease.' This promise was followed by a covenant that such a great flood would never occur again, and this was confirmed by the sign of a rainbow: 'When I bring clouds over the earth and the bow is seen in the clouds, I will remember my covenant that is between me and you and every living creature of all flesh. And the waters shall never again become a flood to destroy all flesh. When the bow is in the clouds, I will see it and remember the everlasting covenant between God and every living creature of all flesh that is on the earth' (Genesis 9:14–16). Believers do not take the seasons for granted, but appreciate them as a gift from God, and are joyful that a bright spring returns after a long dark cold winter, and that there will be a warm summer to follow.

Nuclear holocaust?

There have been times in the more recent past when man's greatest fear has not been from a global flood, but from an imminent nuclear holocaust, or apocalypse. This happened during the Cuban missile crisis in October 1962. The Soviet leader, Nikita Khrushchev, had begun installing medium- and intermediate-range nuclear ballistic missiles at the request of Fidel Castro in Cuba. The American President J. F. Kennedy, after intense negotiations, agreed to withdraw US missiles from Italy and Turkey in return for the withdrawal of the Soviet missiles from Cuba. From that moment, a hotline was established between Washington and Moscow to help prevent such a catastrophe ever occurring, which could have wiped out all life on Earth. It was of comfort in those days to remember our Lord's words: 'Just as it was in the days of Noah, so will it be in the days of the Son of Man. They were eating and drinking and marrying and being given in marriage, until the day when Noah entered the ark, and the flood came and destroyed them all ... so will it be on the day when the Son of Man is revealed' (Luke 17:26–27, 30). Jesus is saying that when he returns at the end of time, to save his people and judge the world, men

and women will be still going about their normal pursuits, going out for meals with their families and enjoying life's pleasures. They will not have been destroyed in a global nuclear war, but many will be careless about their souls and must face God's judgement.

Babel and beyond

We are continuing to follow the early history of the way mankind has used the space God gave them on planet Earth. After Noah and his family had settled on dry land, God repeated the command he originally gave to Adam and Eve: 'Be fruitful and multiply and fill the earth' (Genesis 9:1). They had no problem with being fruitful, but were reluctant about filling the earth. This was understandable. They all had family ties, and there is a comfort in belonging to a social network, of knowing your roots and the places with which you are familiar. They had, however, outgrown the area in which they had initially settled, so decided to move westward *en masse* to a more suitable large plain area.

This plain was in the land of Shinar, which became Babylonia and eventually modern-day Iraq. It was the beginning of the Sumerian culture, arguably the oldest civilisation in the world.[10] The leaders came up with a proposal: 'And they said to one another, "Come, let us make bricks, and burn them thoroughly." And they had brick for stone, and bitumen for mortar. Then they said, "Come, let us build ourselves a city and a tower with its top in the heavens, and let us make a name for ourselves, lest we be dispersed over the face of the whole earth"' (Genesis 11:3–4). This shows two things: they were not living in mud huts, but had made advances in building technology and developed strong bricks which were bound together with a bituminous compound; secondly, they were determined to resist God's express command to spread out over the face of the earth.

---

[10] https://en.wikipedia.org/wiki/Sumer

2: Space

The building of a tower was not simply merely to provide an exhibition piece to show how clever they were, like the Eiffel tower which has since become the symbol of Paris. It was to have a distinctly religious significance. They thought they could reach up to God's dwelling place and become like God, just as Satan had tempted Eve that she could 'be like God' (Genesis 3:5). Henry Morris (1918–2006) has described how astrology developed from careful astronomical observations, and the common signs of the zodiac can be traced back to Mesopotamia.[11]

THEY SAID, 'COME, LET US BUILD OURSELVES A CITY AND A TOWER WITH ITS TOP IN THE HEAVENS, AND LET US MAKE A NAME FOR OURSELVES, LEST WE BE DISPERSED OVER THE FACE OF THE WHOLE EARTH.'

~ GENESIS 11:3 – 4 ~

Nimrod, the great-grandson of Noah, became the first king of the post-Flood world at Babel and was a mighty hunter who went on to found other cities, like Nineveh. Either he or his father, Cush, took responsibility for building the tower, which would have taken the form of a *ziggurat*, and which became a common structure in cities of that region of Mesopotamia. Essentially there was a foundation of a long flight of steps or terraces leading up to a temple at the top. Here they would worship a whole pantheon of gods and minor gods, especially An (the god of heaven), Utu (the sun god) and Sin (the moon god).[12]

---

[11] Henry M. Morris: *The Long War against God*, Baker Book House, 1989, 246-248)
[12] https://en.wikipedia.org/wiki/Sumer#Temples_and_temple_organisation

God later warned the Israelites: 'And beware lest you raise your eyes to heaven, and when you see the sun and the moon and the stars, all the host of heaven, you be drawn away and bow down to them and serve them' (Deuteronomy 4:19a). His anger against the rebellious people at Babel was to confuse their language. The parts of their brains responsible for speech were reprogrammed so that some families were given a new language which other families could not understand. This meant they could not work together as previously, and so they decided that the best option was to branch out and form their own communities in ever-widening circles. This event led to the many nations and languages throughout the world.

'AND BEWARE LEST YOU RAISE YOUR EYES TO HEAVEN, AND WHEN YOU SEE THE SUN AND THE MOON AND THE STARS, ALL THE HOST OF HEAVEN, YOU BE DRAWN AWAY AND BOW DOWN TO THEM AND SERVE THEM.'

~ DEUTERONOMY 4:19 ~

2: Space

God's remoteness and nearness

Having examined the vastness of the universe and how we have come to have our own language and culture, inhabiting a small corner on this speck of dust we call Earth, we could be forgiven in imagining that God must be remote, separate and distinct from his universe. We must remember, however, that he is not made from the dust of the ground or the elements of the periodic table as we are. On the other hand, we read that he is aware of all that goes on upon our planet, and all that people are thinking in their hearts.

It is difficult to view the infinite God with reference to space. The theologian Louis Berkhof describes the 'immensity' of God as 'that perfection of the Divine Being by which He transcends all spatial limitations, and yet is present in every point of space with His whole Being.'[13]

THE IMMENSITY OF GOD

'... THAT PERFECTION OF THE DIVINE BEING BY WHICH HE TRANSCENDS ALL SPATIAL LIMITATIONS, AND YET IS PRESENT IN EVERY POINT OF SPACE WITH HIS WHOLE BEING.'

~ LOUIS BERKHOF ~

(Note: The 'immensity' of God is usually called his transcendence, whereas the fact that God is equally present everywhere is called his immanence or omnipresence.)

The old hymnist John Mason (c. 1646–1694) described the greatness, eternity and omnipresence of God as follows:

---

[13] Louis Berkhof, *Systematic Theology*, Banner of Truth, London, 1966 (reprint), p. 60

How great a being Lord is Thine,
Which doth all beings keep!
Thy knowledge is the only line
To sound so vast a deep.
Thou art a sea without a shore,
A sun without a sphere;
Thy time is now and evermore,
Thy place is everywhere.

David's view of God

David was the King of Israel, but also a prophet and poet. He was brought up as a shepherd boy, and would have spent nights out in the open and noticed the stars sparkling in the night sky. He was very aware of the presence of God: 'Even though I walk through the valley of the shadow of death, I will fear no evil, for you are with me; your rod and your staff they comfort me' (Psalm 23:4). In Psalm 139:2, David ponders the fact of God's omniscience: 'You know me when I sit down and when I rise up; you discern my thoughts from afar.' Yet although he knew God was right there with him, he was also aware that God both made and filled the universe.

WHAT IS MAN THAT YOU ARE MINDFUL OF HIM, AND THE SON OF MAN THAT YOU CARE FOR HIM?

~ PSALM 8:3 ~

David ponders: 'When I look at your heavens, the work of your fingers, the moon and the stars, which you have set in place, what is man that you are mindful of him, and the son of man that you care for him? ... You have given him dominion over the works of your hands; you have put all things under his feet'

2: Space

(Psalm 8:3–4, 6). We see here that David also saw his responsibility to care for the creation in the same way as God had commanded Adam. The author of Psalm 113 exclaims: 'From the rising of the sun to its setting, the name of the LORD is to be praised! The LORD is high above all nations, and his glory above the heavens! Who is like the LORD our God who is seated on high, who looks far down on the heavens and the earth?' (vv. 3–6).

God is therefore shown to be both high above the heavens and yet simultaneously with his people on Earth. The most amazing truth is that God's own Son, the Lord Jesus Christ, came personally to this planet at his incarnation, and bridged the great divide between the holiness of Heaven and the sinfulness of Earth. The godly Methodist hymn writer Charles Wesley (1707–1788) marvelled at this truth when he wrote: 'Our God contracted to a span, incomprehensibly made man' (Charles Wesley, *Let earth and Heaven combine*).

> GOD'S OWN SON, THE LORD JESUS CHRIST, CAME PERSONALLY TO THIS PLANET AT HIS INCARNATION, AND BRIDGED THE GREAT DIVIDE BETWEEN THE HOLINESS OF HEAVEN AND THE SINFULNESS OF EARTH.

My space

It's all very well roaming the universe and seeing how our tiny planet of Earth fits into the vast scheme of things, but how does this knowledge affect you and me personally? We may well be an infinitesimally small dot on the page of an immeasurably large universe but, according to the Bible, we are not insignificant or meaningless. We have a vital part to play in God's plan for how the history of the world will fulfil his purposes. It is time to consider whether we are giving God the space in our hearts and lives that he desires, stemming from his love for us.

Breathing space

There is no doubt that the pace of life and pressures of modern work practices are greater than ever before. There is a strong competitiveness in education constraining students to achieve better grades in their exams, and schools to excel in the results tables. This is all intended to allow students to be able to proceed to the university of their choice, and then on to lucrative and rewarding careers. This engenders much stress in trying to fulfil the expectations of one's parents and teachers. Tragically, some bright students, even at top universities, take their own lives because they think they are failures. They unfortunately miss the perspective that there is a meaningful and vital world which exists outside the university system, and lack the ability to choose to opt out of academia and use their other talents in a creative way because of a fear that they will disappoint their family sponsors. Some great inventors, like Michael Faraday and Thomas Edison, and leaders like Horatio Nelson and Winston Churchill, or preachers like Charles Haddon Spurgeon, never attended university; in fact, it might have dulled their original minds. If you are in the position of being uncertain whether you should pursue a university degree, take a breathing space, and consider where you could be most fulfilled, while earning enough at least to cover basic expenses.

Left: Spurgeon; Right: Churchill

2: Space

Perhaps you have left college and find yourself in the role of a trainee IT specialist, accountant, lawyer or doctor, for example. You have 'arrived', but it is not working out quite as you expected. There is the early start with a long commute each day, you are often expected to work anti-social hours and take work home to finish on the laptop. There are emails in the evening from your senior manager asking you to get your data sheets ready for tomorrow's meeting which has been brought forward. All these stresses add up to increased tension in one's family or social life.

> SOME GREAT INVENTORS, LIKE MICHAEL FARADAY AND THOMAS EDISON, AND LEADERS LIKE HORATIO NELSON AND WINSTON CHURCHILL, OR PREACHERS LIKE CHARLES HADDON SPURGEON, NEVER ATTENDED UNIVERSITY.

Added to all the above is the continuing possibility of job cuts. Perhaps the sacking of a whole level of middle-managers in a restructuring scheme will devolve their jobs onto the lower grades, increasing their workload still further. Some people are pretty sanguine about all this and seem to be able to cope without going under. Others simply crack up through no fault of their own— they have just been pushed beyond their breaking point. Perhaps they see how the situation is developing and come to a decision before they become ill or their family is suffering too much from this over-demanding work routine. Having budgeted carefully, they decide that they will 'escape to the country'. The BBC programme with this title often depicts people who feel they must escape the rat race of life in London. They must have some breathing space, which may mean a simplified lifestyle, but they will have more quality time together. It is using the 'space' God has given in a healing and fulfilling way and, especially for the believer, making it easier to leave the materialistic gods of the world behind. Perhaps now they can be themselves and express the diversity of their talents and personalities.

Tiredness can kill
One's best plan might be to stay put, but change the nature of one's employment. Whether we stay or go, we all need regular breaks. In the 1990s, a sign appeared on our motorways: 'Tiredness can kill — Take a break.' Jesus and his disciples had a gruelling schedule; they often walked miles in the hot sun, travelling from place to place to minister to the people. He once said to them: '"Come away by yourselves to a desolate place and rest a while." For many were coming and going, and they had no leisure even to eat' (Mark 6:31). We don't necessarily have to escape to the country, but we need to have a quiet time each day to refresh both body and soul.

Jesus advises us to pray: 'But when you pray, go into your room and shut the door and pray to your Father who is in secret. And your Father who sees in secret will reward you' (Matthew 6:6). This is not always easy when babies and young children come into our lives, but a session alone can usually be snatched at some point in the day for a Bible reading with meditation and prayer. It is sur- 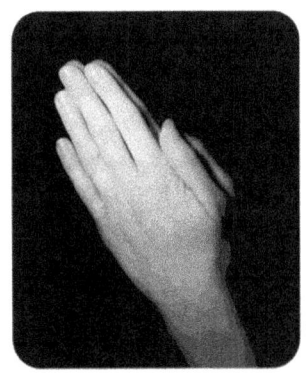 prising how refreshing this can be. When King David was being hunted down by his enemies in the Judean wilderness, he found it difficult to find a quiet place on his own, but he wrote: 'I remember you upon my bed, and meditate on you in the watches of the night' (Psalm 63:6). Where there is a will, there is a way. The author of Psalm 121 found great comfort and help in lifting up his eyes to the hills, and Mount Zion in particular. This was where God met with his people, first in David's tabernacle (2 Samuel

2: Space

6:17), then in the temple built by Solomon. He writes: 'My help comes from the LORD, who made heaven and earth. He will not let your foot be moved; he who keeps you will not slumber... The LORD will keep you from all evil; he will keep your life' (vs. 2, 3 & 7). What a great promise to carry with us throughout the day as we encounter life's many problems: financial, work-related, and possibly personal or involving family relationships.

Find a space

Whether we thrive in the city or in the country, we need to find a space to take time and think. This book is about subjects which raise questions in our minds. We may have briefly considered them, but then they have been relegated to our subconscious. They seem too vast and complicated to affect our everyday lives, and yet their shadow haunts us continuously. What is the purpose of the universe, our world—and where are we at the moment? Is there any sense in it all; am I alone in time and space, and what lies in the future?

'... THESE ARE ALL INADEQUATE, BECAUSE THE INFINITE ABYSS CAN ONLY BE FILLED BY AN INFINITE AND IMMUTABLE OBJECT, THAT IS TO SAY, ONLY BY GOD HIMSELF.'

~ BLAISE PASCAL ~

Inner space

People pay a lot of attention, and money, to exploring outer space, but perhaps our inner space deserves some investigating, too. There is an inner void deep in our souls which can only be satisfied if filled with God. Blaise Pascal (1623–1662), the French mathematician, physicist and inventor, famously once commented on this phenomenon: 'What is it then that this desire and this inability proclaim to us, but that there was once in man a true happiness of which there now remain to him only the mark and empty trace, which he in vain tries to fill from all his surroundings, seeking from things absent the help he does not obtain in things present? But these are all inadequate, because the infinite abyss can only be filled by an infinite and immutable object, that is to say, only by God Himself.'[14]

Pascal later comments: 'If it is a sign of weakness to prove God by nature, do not despise Scripture; if it is a sign of strength to have known these contradictions, esteem Scripture.'[15] Here is another great mind which revered the Scriptures, as we are endeavouring to do. Augustine is known for his saying that 'You have made us for yourself, O Lord, and our hearts are restless until they rest in you.' He wrote this at the end of the very first paragraph of his *Confessions*. He was aware of this inner angst, a sense that something is missing—that something which is God. We all need to find God.

The writer of *Ecclesiastes*, probably Solomon, the wisest man who has ever lived, wrote: 'I have seen the business that God has given to the children of man to be busy with. He has made everything beautiful in its time. Also, he has put eternity into man's heart, yet so that he cannot find out what God has done from the beginning to the end' (Ecclesiastes 3:10–11). He has detected this inner void, a sense of eternity, but also that we lack the ability to understand everything about the universe.

---

[14] *Pascal's Pensées*, Introduction by T. S. Eliot, Dutton, New York, 1958, section 425; accessed at: http://www.gutenberg.org/files/18269/18269-h/18269-h.htm
[15] *ibid.* section 428

2: Space

> 'YOU HAVE MADE US FOR YOURSELF, O LORD,
> AND OUR HEARTS ARE RESTLESS UNTIL THEY
> REST IN YOU.'
>
> ~ AUGUSTINE ~

People were still searching for something spiritual to fill this vacuum in their lives at the time the apostle Paul was walking the streets of Athens. He wrote: 'For as I passed along and observed the objects of your worship, I found also an altar with this inscription, "To the unknown god." What therefore you worship as unknown, this I proclaim to you. The God who made the world and everything in it, being Lord of heaven and earth, does not live in temples made by man, nor is he served by human hands, as though he needed anything, since he himself gives to all mankind life and breath and everything. And he made from one man every nation of mankind to live on all the face of the earth, having determined allotted periods and the boundaries of their dwelling place, that they should seek God, and perhaps feel their way toward him and find him. Yet he is actually not far from each one of us, for "In him we live and move and have our being"; as even some of your own poets have said, "For we are indeed his offspring"' (Acts 17:23–28).

Who is in control?
Paul has made sense of the universe, or we should rather say that God has revealed this truth to him. He saw that it is God who gives us life and breath, and determines our time and space, 'the boundaries of our dwelling place'. What a peace and security this brings into our lives!

The Jews were trusting in their religious practices and traditions to save them, but here in Athens the Greeks, like the Romans, put their faith in their gods. The trouble was that there were so many gods that they were frightened that they might offend one of these deities by omitting to make a shrine in its honour—hence the shrine 'To the unknown God'. In their homes, the Greeks would have a shrine to Hestia, goddess of the hearth. The Romans also had their Lares Familiares. Today in India, Hindus customarily have their household shrines, containing a Murti, an image believed to be inhab-  ited by a deity. Offerings are made to it, and also to dead ancestors. In some predominantly Roman Catholic areas of America, like Kentucky and Indiana, garden shrines called 'bathtub madonnas' can be seen. A half-buried bathtub provides a setting for a Madonna. Statues of the Virgin Mary are a common sight across Europe, especially the wayside Madonnas at the side of the road and in vineyards, presumably to bless the grape harvest.

> WE CANNOT RESIST READING THE DAILY HOROSCOPES IN THE NEWSPAPER OR TOUCHING WOOD FOR GOOD LUCK AND PERHAPS CROSSING OUR FINGERS AS WELL.

Would we mentally attribute the course of our lives to a man-made image, or to the living God—the creator of the universe? Perhaps we consider that we are too sophisticated and technologically advanced to consider setting up shrines in our modern apartments and flats. Instead, we cannot resist reading the daily horoscopes in the newspaper or touching wood for good luck and perhaps crossing our fingers as well. It is reported that many businesses in India consult astrologers before launching a new product to make sure it coincides with an auspicious date.[16]

Fill up

Even if we would never do such things, we have to fill our inner space, Pascal's 'infinite abyss', with something. Generally we tend to fill our thoughts and plans for the future with our own ambitions. That is not to say we don't spend time helping others in some way; it is that we do so only if it suits us and gives us pleasure, a kind of inner glow. The Christian finds a deeper inner satisfaction by seeking what God's will would be in any situation. Solomon advises us: 'In all your ways acknowledge him, and he will make straight your paths' (Proverbs 3:6). His father David would have taught him: 'Trust in the LORD, and do good; dwell in the land and be‑  friend faithfulness. Delight yourself in the LORD, and he will give you the desires of your heart. Commit your way to the LORD; trust in him, and he will act' (Psalm 37:3–5). David said it should be a delight to live our lives under God's love and guidance.

Jesus will fill us with his Spirit

Elsewhere David says: '[Y]ou anoint my head with oil; my cup overflows' (Psalm 23:5b). God filled him with good things, and here the oil he refers to is a symbol of the Holy Spirit, and reminded David of when he was anointed king. At the time of the Last Supper, when Jesus was about to leave his disciples, he told them: 'These things I have spoken to you, that my joy may be in

---

[16] http://www.bbc.co.uk/news/business-25971921

you, and that your joy may be full' (John 15:11).

Through reading and heeding the words of Scripture, especially our Lord's words, we will be on the right track to find an inner joy and peace. Jesus said earlier: '"Whoever believes in me, as the Scripture has said, 'Out of his heart will flow rivers of living water.'" Now this he said about the Spirit, whom those who believed in him were to receive, for as yet the Spirit had not been given, because Jesus was not yet glorified' (John:7:38–39). This is the true meaning of spirituality, and it begins with believing in Jesus and then praying to 'Our Father in heaven' (Matthew 6:9–13) that he would forgive our sins and help us lead a life pleasing to him.

THROUGH READING AND HEEDING THE WORDS OF SCRIPTURE, ESPECIALLY OUR LORD'S WORDS, WE WILL BE ON THE RIGHT TRACK TO FIND AN INNER JOY AND PEACE.

3

LIFE

Then the L ORD God formed the man of dust from the ground and breathed into his nostrils the breath of life, and the man became a living creature.

Genesis 2:7

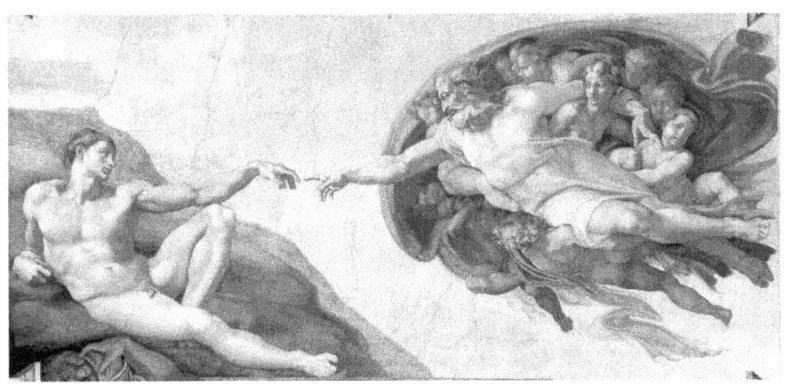

3: Life

Life could be considered as the whole history of civilization, with the triumphs of its medical, educational and scientific achievements, and the exploration of this planet and beyond into space. There would be the sad record of the many wars and cruel murders, the slavery and persecutions, and the martyrdom of holy men by burning them alive in the cities of Britain in 1555. To describe all of this would take an encyclopaedia larger than any house could accommodate, or a computer file so large it would swallow up all the available memory and a whole lifetime would be insufficient for anyone to read it.

WHAT WE ARE MAINLY CONCERNED WITH IN THIS CHAPTER IS HOW LIVING CREATURES, ESPECIALLY OURSELVES, CAME TO EXIST ON PLANET EARTH.

What we are mainly concerned with in this chapter is how living creatures, especially ourselves, came to exist on planet Earth. Present knowledge from space exploration has yet to detect any life-form whatsoever on any other planet or other object in outer space. Apart from on Earth, the rest of the universe consists of inorganic rocks and dust, gases and liquefied gases. Why is our planet so different, where did we come from, and is there a 'purpose' in life?

Origins

As mentioned earlier in the chapter on Time, the only possible way for us to obtain any definite facts or knowledge about the beginning of the universe, or of the origin of life on earth, is if an objective observer were present at the event and were outside of the system where the event was occurring. This knowledge would need to be revealed to the intelligent beings that were now living in the newly formed universe on planet Earth. This information would have to be accepted in good faith, and seen over time to be a reasonable explanation when compared to all they observe in the world around them.

WE HAVE FOUND THE BIBLE TO BE THE MOST CREDIBLE AND RELIABLE EXPLANATION OF ORIGINS, SATISFYING NOT ONLY TO BOTH REASON AND OBSERVATION, BUT ALSO FROM PRACTISING THE TEACHINGS OF THE SCRIPTURES AND EXPERIENCING THE TRANSFORMING POWER OF THE HOLY SPIRIT.

We have found the Bible to be the most credible and reliable explanation of origins, satisfying not only to both reason and observation, but also from practising the teachings of the Scriptures and experiencing the transforming power of the Holy Spirit in our lives. They are reliable historically, and this is confirmed by many archaeological discoveries of events described in the Bible. It is not mythology or a grand fairytale, but rooted in history and is true. No attack on its truth or historical accuracy has ever been upheld. Having said that, the Bible is not a history text-book, so events might be recorded according to themes, rather than chronological succession, and care must be taken in the interpretation of some passages. It speaks rather of the nature of God and the nature of mankind and our duties towards him. The origin of life and its

3: Life

immediate aftermath is an important part of this revelation, and is found in the first book of the Bible, Genesis, and particularly in the first three chapters.

> NO ATTACK ON THE BIBLE'S TRUTH OR
> HISTORICAL ACCURACY HAS EVER BEEN UPHELD.

Origin of matter

Living plants and creatures are made of matter, but where did matter come from? Did it simply come from a Big Bang? But that begs the question: where did the energy or super-energetic particle come from which exploded with this Big Bang? If so, it seems to be at variance with the Law of Conservation of Mass (or Matter) regarding a chemical reaction, which can be stated thus:

In a chemical reaction, matter is neither created nor destroyed.

It was discovered, or at least formulated, by Antoine Laurent Lavoisier (1743–94) in about 1785. In 1842, Julius Robert Mayer discovered the similar Law of Conservation of Energy, which is now called the First Law of Thermodynamics and says:

Energy is neither created nor destroyed.

Following Albert Einstein's discovery of the equation $E = mc^2$, the two laws were merged into the Law of Conservation of Mass-Energy:

The total amount of mass and energy in the universe is constant.

Einstein commented:

Energy cannot be created or destroyed; it can only be changed from one form to another.

3: Life

'BY FAITH WE UNDERSTAND THAT THE UNIVERSE WAS CREATED BY THE WORD OF GOD, SO THAT WHAT IS SEEN WAS NOT MADE OUT OF THINGS THAT ARE VISIBLE.'

~ HEBREWS 11.3 ~

This boils down to the observation that once our present universe had come into existence, its total mass-energy has remained constant. Furthermore, the present universe had to have been initially created out of nothing in order for it to begin to exist. Apart from a supernatural intervention creating *ex nihilo*, it could not have suddenly appeared at an event where there was no previously existing energy-particle. If there was a pre-existing concentration of energy or energy and mass, then the so-called 'Big Bang' could not have been the beginning. So the Creationist maintains a logical position when claiming that the universe was initially created, while acknowledging it is subsequently expanding from its original size.

We noted previously that no-one was present at the beginning of the universe, so we just have to rely on God's revelation—the alternative is to have faith in unprovable hypotheses. 'By faith we understand that the universe was created by the word of God, so that what is seen was not made out of things that are visible' (Hebrews 11.3).

Origin of life

If we try and use our own reasoning powers to construct a theory of the origin of life, we will come up with all sorts of strange and improbable ideas. If the proponent of a theory is a famous person, then this idea will be in favour for a generation or so, but then be replaced by the next popular concept. One can have no faith in a merely human hypothesis, which is sure to be superseded by another improved one which seeks to keep pace with the development of scientific knowledge. The divinely revealed account of the origin of the world and all of the life on our planet has stood the test of time, and nothing has been disproved and shown to be an impossible event.

Classical theories of origins

Some of the most intelligent people in the ancient world must surely have been the Greeks. They may well have been unaware of the account of the creation of the world and of living beings as recorded in the book of Genesis. Using all the powers of reason and knowledge, they come up with ideas which, compared to the concise sequential account with running commentary as found in Genesis chapters 1 to 3, appear quite fanciful, even absurd.

Thales of Miletus

Thales (639–544 BC) lived in Asia Minor, present-day Turkey, around the time that the Israelites were enduring their 70-year captivity in Babylon. He observed that water was the most prevalent substance on the planet, and was necessary for the survival of all plant and animal life. He therefore postulated that life must have originated in the sea, although he had no definite evidence for this. His pupil was Anaximander of Miletus (c. 610—c. 546 BC), who tried to refine his master's idea. He believed that the spontaneous generation of life had occurred in the mud and mist while the water was being evaporated by the heat of the sun. He  reckoned that this in itself was inadequate to generate life, and that there needed to be a vital force, or immortal ethereal substance, which he called *apeiron* ('having no limit'). Eventually this led to the formation of a fishlike creature which conceived a potential man and woman in its belly. It finally burst open and deposited them on the land.[1]

If Anaximander was correct, this hapless couple would have had no idea of what they were doing there, or their purpose in life. Neither would they have had the comfort of being supported by a personal God who loved them and provided for them.

---

[1] http://www.yale.edu/ynhti/curriculum/units/1980/5/80.05.11.x.html

About 600 years after Anaximander, the apostle Paul visited both Miletus and Ephesus, which was about a 37-mile sea journey to the north. In his letter to the Ephesians (2:12), he recalled how he had found them before they believed the gospel and exhorted them: 'Remember that you were at that time separated from Christ, alienated from the commonwealth of Israel and strangers to the covenants of promise, having no hope and without God in the world.'

HUMANITY, ACTING AND THINKING WITHOUT REFERRING TO GOD'S REVELATION, WILL END UP IN AN INCREASINGLY DARK AND TERRIFYING PLACE.

On the other hand, the Israelites had all the benefits of God's revelation to them through the prophets, informing them of his own character and their origin in Adam, together with their corresponding duties, the future advent of a Messiah-Saviour, and their final destiny of dwelling with God in his kingdom for ever. They had rejected God's revealed will for them, worshipped the manmade gods of the surrounding nations, and so ended up in captivity to be taught obedience. If we feel all alone in the world, perhaps we should seek the Son of God who, the apostle Paul said, 'loved me and gave himself for me' (Galatians 2:20b). As we proceed through history, we will see that humanity, acting and thinking without referring to God's revelation, will end up in an increasingly dark and terrifying place.

Plato, Aristotle and Epicurus

Plato, Aristotle, Epicurus

Plato (428–348 BC) introduced the concept of the Demiurge in *Timaeus*, (ca. 360 BC), a work speculating on the nature of the physical world, which he considered a living thing with body and soul. This Demiurge was considered to be an artisan creator god, which fashioned the universe out of the chaotic material which had been already produced by a Supreme Being. This impersonal 'prime mover' was later personified as Zeus. It is interesting that a thousand years earlier, Moses, who wrote the Pentateuch (the first five books of the Bible, also known as the Book of the Law — Deuteronomy 31:9 and Joshua 1:8), recorded that the earth was formed out of a state of being formless and empty, or in a state of chaos. This was the thought that inspired the hymn writer John Marriott (1780–1825) when he wrote:

> *Thou whose almighty word*
> *Chaos and darkness heard,*
> *And took their flight,*
> *Hear us we humbly pray,*
> *And where the gospel day*
> *Sheds not its glorious ray,*
> *Let there be light!*

3: Life

Just as the light of creation dispelled the primeval darkness and disorder, Marriott, a First Class Honours graduate from Christ Church, Oxford, and tutor to the family of the Duke of Buccleuch, also wanted the light of the gospel to dispel the moral darkness and ignorance of Christianity from those further parts of the world which were being opened up to exploration and trade.

ARISTOTLE BELIEVED THAT CREATURES WERE ARRANGED IN A GRADED SCALE OF PERFECTION RISING FROM PLANTS ON UP TO MAN.

Plato was surpassed in importance by his pupil Aristotle (384 BC—322 BC), who believed that creatures were arranged in a graded scale of perfection rising from plants on up to man, the *scala naturae*, the Ladder of Life or Great Chain of Being.[2][3] This was to reappear in a more complex form in Darwin's Tree of Life.

A century and a half later, Epicurus (ca. 341–ca. 270 BC), declared that only matter was real, pleasure is the sole intrinsic good, and there is no divine intervention. Variations on these ideas bubble up again during the eighteenth and nineteenth centuries.

---

[2] Ernst Mayr, *The Growth of Biological Thought*, 1982, pp 201-202

[3] Arthur O. Lovejoy, *The Great Chain of Being*, Harvard, (1936)

Classical Roman philosophy

Two hundred years later, Lucretius (ca. 96–53 BC), wrote in *De Rerum Natura*: 'The earth, which generated every living species and once brought forth from its womb the bodies of huge beasts, has now scarcely strength to generate animalcules. For I assume that the races of mortal creatures were not let down into the fields from heaven by a golden cord, nor generated from the sea or the rock-bearing surf, but born of the same earth that now provides their nurture…' Lucretius's philosophy denied life after death and the existence of any divinity concerned with man's welfare. He held to a kind of spontaneous generation of species, but the main result is that God is left out of the reckoning.

LUCRETIUS HELD TO A KIND OF SPONTANEOUS GENERATION OF SPECIES, BUT THE MAIN RESULT IS THAT GOD IS LEFT OUT OF THE RECKONING.

Augustine and Aquinas

Augustine (AD 353–430) tried to reconcile the accepted views of the old Greek philosophers concerning the origins of life with the biblical account, and so he imagined a progressive development in creation: 'For all these things were created at the beginning ... but they await the proper opportunity for their appearance.' This is now called theistic evolution, and shows the influence of Plato. Comments on this theory are given at the end of this chapter.

Thomas Aquinas (1225–1274) believed in the divine origin of the Scriptures, but sought to allegorise Genesis to fit in with the Greek pantheistic philosophy of Aristotle. He thus put the 'light of reason' on a par with 'the light of grace'. Copernicus (1473–1543) and Galileo (1564–1642) both believed the biblical record of origins, but their heliocentric system had to overcome Aristotelianism before it could be accepted.

The Great Awakening

The great Evangelical Awakening in the mid-eighteenth century under John and Charles Wesley (1703–1791; 1707–1788), and George Whitefield (pictured) (1714–1770) in England, and Daniel Rowland (1711–1790), Howel Harris (1714–1773) and William Williams (Pantycelyn) (1717–1791) in Wales, affected tens of thousands of working-class families and some of the higher classes like Lady Selina Hastings, Countess of Huntingdon (1707–1791). Most of the upper echelons of society, however, remained aloof from such 'enthusiasm'. By the turn of the century, the more philosophically and scientifically minded religious people among the favoured classes had adopted the Socinianism or Unitarianism, which was popular with the educated elite.

Joseph Priestley

Joseph Priestley (1733–1804), a discoverer of oxygen, was a theologian-scientist, who started as a Calvinist, but ended challenging the deity of Christ and his virgin birth, and the doctrines of original sin, the atonement, and the Trinity, considering the latter a 'gross corruption of Christianity'.[4]

In spite of his unorthodox views, it is remarkable that Priestley should defend the biblical account of Creation in his book: *Institutes of Natural and Revealed Religion*:[5]

> Objections have been made to the Mosaic account of the creation, and the general deluge. But even in these cases the history of Moses is found to supply a more probable hypothesis, to account for the present state of things, than any other that has yet been proposed; and improvements in philosophy do, upon the whole, rather strengthen than weaken this conclusion.

Priestley adds his view on the creation of human life in his book: *Disquisitions Relating to Matter and* Spirit:[6]

> The doctrine of the scripture is, that God made man of the dust of the ground, and by simply animating this organized matter, made him that living, percipient, and intelligent being that he is. According to revelation, death is a state of rest and insensibility, and our only, though sure hope of a

---

[4] Joseph Priestley, *Disquisitions: The History of the Philosophical Doctrine Concerning the Origin of the Soul, and the Nature of Matter; with its Influence on Christianity, Especially with respect to the Doctrine of the Pre-existence of Christ*, J. Johnson, Birmingham, 1782, p. 400

[5] Joseph Priestley, *Institutes of Natural and Revealed Religion*, Volume 1, J. Johnson, Birmingham, 1782; *The Evidences of Revealed Religion*, Chapter 7, *A View of the Principal Objections to the Jewish and Christian Revelations*, p. 39

[6] Joseph Priestley, *Disquisitions Relating to Matter and Spirit*, Vol. 1, Second Edition, which includes *The History of the Philosophical Doctrine Concerning the Origin of the Soul, and the Nature of Matter; With its Influence on Christianity, Especially with respect to the Doctrine of the Pre-existence of Christ*, pp. 294-295

future life, is founded on the doctrine of the resurrection of the whole man, at some distant period; this assurance being sufficiently confirmed to us, both by the evident tokens of a divine commission attending the persons who delivered the doctrine, and especially by the actual resurrection of Jesus Christ, which is more authentically attested than any other fact in history.

> 'THE RESURRECTION OF JESUS CHRIST ... IS MORE AUTHENTICALLY ATTESTED THAN ANY OTHER FACT IN HISTORY.'
>
> ~ JOSEPH PRIESTLEY ~

He used scientific experience and human reason to judge the validity of Christian doctrine, and therefore allowed man's changing opinions to overrule his assessment of the truth of any Scripture text. Into this atmosphere of revealed religion being made to bow down in submission to the might of human wisdom, we have the arrival of Charles Darwin's grandfather, Erasmus Darwin.

Erasmus Darwin (1731–1802)

Erasmus, the grandfather of Charles Darwin, was a physician, inventor and poet. He laid the foundations of his grandson Charles's theories when he suggested: 'Perhaps all the products of nature are in their progress to greater perfection … consonant to the dignity of the Creator of all things.'[7] In fact, Erasmus anticipated his grandson on almost every point of evolutionary theory apart from natural selection, seen especially in his book *Zoonomia*, first published in 1794, where he said,

> Would it be too bold to imagine that, in the great length of time since the earth began to exist, perhaps millions of ages before the commencement of the history of mankind … all warm-blooded animals have arisen from one living filament, which the great First Cause endued with animality, with the power of acquiring new parts, attended with new propensities, directed by irritations, sensations, volitions and associations, and thus possessing the faculty of continuing to improve by its own inherent activity, and of delivering down these improvements by generation to its posterity, world without end![8]

---

[7] Erasmus Darwin, *The Temple of Nature; or, The Origin of Society*, notes on line 122, Canto 2, *Reproduction of Life*, Part 3, J. Johnson, London, 1803; http://www.gutenberg.org/files/26861/26861-h/26861-h.htm#canto2_l122

[8] Erasmus Darwin, *Zoonomia*, Volume 1, J. Johnson, 1796 (2nd edn.), London, Section XXXIX, Of Generation, IV.8; http://www.gutenberg.org/files/15707/15707-h/15707-h.htm

3: Life

Erasmus Darwin's final long poem, *The Temple of Nature*, originally titled *The Origin of Society*, was published posthumously in 1803 and centres on his newly-conceived theory of evolution. It traces the progression of life from micro-organisms to civilised society. He admits to an impersonal Great First Cause, which is little different from Plato's Demiurge, and which wound up the world, then stood back to let it develop according to chance events. In contrast, the Bible speaks of a God who created the universe, with mankind being a finished and perfect creature made in the image of God; the first people were a climax to the Creation and possessed souls capable of loving and worshipping their Creator and enjoying the surrounding creation, of which they were made stewards. From the very beginning, people had an awareness of their origins and a sense of purpose in life.

[CHARLES] DARWIN HAD BECOME AN AGNOSTIC, MORE IN THE TRADITION OF CLASSICAL PAGAN PHILOSOPHY THAN BIBLICAL CHRISTIANITY.

Charles Robert Darwin

Studying theology at Christ's College, Cambridge, Charles Darwin (1809–1882) was greatly impressed by Paley's *Evidences of Christianity* and his *Natural Theology* (which argues for the existence of God from design). However, by 1880, he confessed to a correspondent, 'I am sorry to have to inform you that I do not believe in the Bible as a divine revelation, and therefore not in Jesus Christ as the Son of God.'[9]

Darwin had become an agnostic, more in the tradition of classical pagan philosophy than biblical Christianity. The influence of the 'higher criticism' movement had crossed the channel from Germany and had a devastating effect on orthodox Christian theology. The authorship and historicity of the Bible was in the melting pot and an aura of doubt hung over all 66 books, leaving a vacuum of unbelief.

It was in this climate that Baden Powell (1796–1860) expressed the view that Christianity should be based on the morality of the New Testament, and that we should abandon the Genesis account of creation. He accepted the authority of God's word on moral issues, but denied it's truthfulness concerning God's works of a physical nature. Furthermore, he denied all possibility of miracles because these would be breaking God's

---

[9] John M. Brentnall, and Russell M. Grigg, *Was Darwin a Christian?*, 2002, quoted in http://christiananswers.net/q-aig/darwin.html

3: Life

physical laws present in the world from its beginning. This is, of course, denying God the right to intervene and override the normal course of events in order to carry out his own purposes which would be to his glory.

Baden Powell's views were expressed in his contribution to *Essays and Reviews*, Ed. J. W. Parker, 1860.[10] It backed up the views of Charles Darwin who had published his *On the Origin of Species by Means of Natural Selection*, in November 1859.[11] His *Origin* largely ignored the Bible and, although not wishing to offend any orthodox Anglican readers, Darwin's conclusion—that mankind had descended from apes or ape-like creatures—could not be avoided. The *Origin of Species* contains just one diagram, the Tree of Life, which had its origins in Aristotle. This simply shows the upper branches and twigs, apparently demonstrating how natural adaptation leads to a variety of species developing out of a genus. Darwin's diagram does not show the relationship between man and the lower animals, but the text fills us in with his ideas.

> THE INFLUENCE OF THE 'HIGHER CRITICISM' MOVEMENT HAD CROSSED THE CHANNEL FROM GERMANY AND HAD A DEVASTATING EFFECT ON ORTHODOX CHRISTIAN THEOLOGY.

In the century from Priestley, we have come from a scientist who doubted some of the fundamental Christian doctrines, yet believed in a God of Creation and a universal flood, (as he admits in *Disquisitions Relating to Matter and Spirit* [p159]—'this flood took place, and almost the whole race of mankind was destroyed by it')—to a scientist who doubted the whole of God's revealed word,

---

[10] https://en.wikipedia.org/wiki/Baden_Powell_(mathematician)
[11] Charles Darwin, *On the Origin of Species by Means of Natural Selection*, John Murray, London, 1859; http://www.gutenberg.org/ebooks/1228

apart from those bits advocating moral principles of which he approved. By using a fallible human reason to interpret his studies on the fossil record and the shape and structure of animals, even though his observations were meticulous, his conclusions were at variance with the Genesis record. By introducing the false dichotomy between God's word and works, Charles Darwin was setting out on a path along which others would follow, leading to dangerous consequences.

Eugenics

Although God favoured the Jews in the matter of revealing himself to them, which he accomplished through the prophets, he had in mind the ultimate goal of encompassing all nations in the scheme of eternal salvation. To further this end, St. Paul was appointed by Christ as an apostle to the Gentiles, to whom he revealed that in the sight of God, 'there is no distinction between Jew and Greek; for the same Lord is Lord of all' (Romans 10:12a). Darwin, however, introduced a racist distinction into his full title to the *Origin of Species*, which was: *On the Origin of Species by Means of Natural Selection, or the Preservation of Favoured Races in the Struggle for Life*. The use of the term 'favoured race' was adopted by the German Nazi movement as applying to their Teutonic race.

GOD HAD IN MIND THE ULTIMATE GOAL OF ENCOMPASSING ALL NATIONS IN THE SCHEME OF ETERNAL SALVATION.

In Darwin's *The Descent of Man*, he shows his belief in the superiority of Europeans over other races: 'The western nations of Europe, who now so immeasurably surpass their former savage progenitors and stand at the summit of civilisation ...'[12] Again he comments: 'At some future period, not very distant as measured by centuries, the civilised races of man will almost certainly exterminate and replace throughout the world the savage races' (*ibid.*, p. 201). This philosophy would open the door to the holocausts of the next century, and is opposite to the Christian spirit of his grandfather, Josiah Wedgewood (1730–1795), who brought public attention to the cause for the abolition of slavery by producing a medallion featuring a slave in chains encircled by the motto: *Am I not a man and a brother*.

HITLER ASSUMED THE RIGHT TO OVERSEE THE EXTERMINATION OF THOSE CONSIDERED TO BE LESS FAVOURED RACES, STARTING WITH THE MURDER OF ABOUT 11 MILLION PEOPLE, INCLUDING 6 MILLION JEWS (IN THE HOLOCAUST) AND THE HANDICAPPED (IN ACTION T4).

In 1925, the leader of the Nazi party, Adolf Hitler (1889–1945), praised and incorporated eugenic ideas in his autobiographical book *Mein Kampf*, and introduced eugenic legislation for the ster-

---

[12] Charles Darwin, *The Descent of Man and Selection in Relation to Sex*, John Murray, London, 1871, p. 178

ilization of 'defectives'. Hitler later assumed it gave him the right to oversee the extermination of those considered to be less favoured races, starting with the murder of about 11 million people, including 6 million Jews (in the Holocaust) and the handicapped (in Action T4). This would mean that the world would eventually be populated by their own super-race who would be left uncontaminated by the less evolved (in their opinion) nations. This holocaust, together with mass sterilization programmes, is the practice of negative eugenics, which eventually leads to inbreeding and the loss of genetic diversity.

Social Darwinism
Although Darwin did not favour enforcing sterilization on anyone, his ideas led to an excuse for the above atrocities. It was his half-cousin Sir Francis Galton (1822–1911) who founded eugenics. Galton considered that social institutions such as welfare and insane asylums were allowing inferior humans to survive and reproduce at levels faster than the more 'superior' humans in respectable society, and if corrections were not soon taken, society would be awash with 'inferiors'. He, and others who came after Darwin, embraced the concept of 'survival of the fittest' and applied it to the acquisition of wealth and status. The same attitude was applied to welfare and charitable giving to the poor in society; it should be curtailed because it was prolonging the survival of the weak to the detriment of the strong.[13]

---

[13] https://en.wikipedia.org/wiki/Social_Darwinism

Marie C. C. Stopes

Marie Stopes (1880–1958) was a clever scientist, a palaeobotanist who studied coal fossils, and was the youngest person to be awarded a D.Sc. by University College, London. She had met Francis Galton as a child and later socially through her family. She campaigned for eugenics after seeing a drop in the birth-rate among the upper and higher middle classes of society and an increase among the lowest classes. The fear was that British society would become burdened with both intellectual and physical weaklings 'as to strangle its economic and military vitality'.[14]

> THE BELIEF AT THE TIME . . . WAS THAT INTELLIGENCE WAS HEREDITARY, SO THE ONLY PERCEIVED REMEDY WAS TO CONTROL THE BIRTH-RATE AMONGST THE LOWER CLASSES.

The belief at the time, and before the arrival of Mendelian genetics, was that intelligence was hereditary, so the only perceived remedy was to control the birth-rate amongst the lower classes. With this is mind, Stopes established the world's first clinic for advising the poorer women on techniques for birth-control. She opposed abortion, calling it 'murder', but those who followed now run it on a business footing in thirty-eight countries, actively

---

[14] Simon R. S. Szreter, *The Genesis of the Registrar-General's Social Classification of Occupations*, The British Journal of Sociology, Vol. 35, No. 4 (Dec., 1984), pp522-546

lobbying for providing facilities for abortion. In 2013 alone, they carried out over three million abortions.[15][16]

The Department of Health has disclosed that for women resident in England and Wales, during 2014: 'The total number of abortions was 184,571. This was 0.4% less than in 2013 (185,311) and 0.6% less than in 2004 (185,713).' In the ten years to 2014 there were a total number of 1,946,240 abortions. We should note that the population of Latvia is 1,971,300.[17][18][19]

> STOPES OPPOSED ABORTION, CALLING IT 'MURDER', BUT THOSE WHO FOLLOWED NOW RUN IT ON A BUSINESS FOOTING IN THIRTY-EIGHT COUNTRIES, ACTIVELY LOBBYING FOR PROVIDING FACILITIES FOR ABORTION.

---

[15] https://mariestopes.org/sites/default/files/Marie_Stopes_International_Global_Impact_Report_2013.pdf#page=7

[16] https://en.wikipedia.org/wiki/Marie_Stopes

[17] https://www.gov.uk/government/uploads/system/uploads/attachment_data/file/433437/2014_Commentary__5_.pdf

[18] https://www.gov.uk/government/statistical-data-sets/abortion-statistics-england-and-wales-2011

[19] https://en.wikipedia.org/wiki/List_of_countries_and_dependencies_by_population

Joseph Stalin

Joseph Stalin (1878–1953) was the leader of the Soviet Union after Lenin's death in 1924 until his own death in 1953. He acted as a virtual dictator, ruthlessly suppressing all opposition. He was brought up in the Georgian Orthodox Church, but led a Communist party which was atheistic in outlook.

A state-approved newspaper, *Bezbozhnik* (Godless or Atheist), was founded in 1922, and helped establish The League of Militant Atheists. The 1929 magazine cover showed muscular workers dumping Jesus from a barrow of garbage, with factories and smoking chimneys in the background. The message was that religion was harmful to the prosperous industrialization of the state. At the Second Congress of Atheists, Nikolai Bukharin, the editor of Pravda, called for the extermination of religion 'at the tip of the bayonet', and Yemelyan Yaroslavsky (1878–1943) declared:

> It is our duty to destroy every religious world-concept... If the destruction of ten million human beings, as happened in the last war, should be necessary for the triumph of one definite class, then that must be done and it will be done.

JOSEPH STALIN WAS BROUGHT UP IN THE GEORGIAN ORTHODOX CHURCH, BUT LED A COMMUNIST PARTY WHICH WAS ATHEISTIC IN OUTLOOK.

Under this sort of governmental ethos, there was a proliferation of executions, transportations to Siberian labour camps with inevitable deaths, and imprisonments—all with hasty mock trials. From 1941–1949 nearly 3.3 million people were deported to Siberia and Central Asia. This was because Stalin mistrusted certain ethnic groups.

In the Ukrainian famine, largely exacerbated by the state's ideological directives, grain produced in the Ukraine was still being exported while its people were starving. The 1932–1933 famine killed from 5 to 10 million people, and the 1947 famine a further 1 to 1.5 million, again largely due to mismanagement of the state's grain reserves. In total, it has been estimated that a minimum of 15 million people were either executed or worked to death in the camps.[20]

---

[20] https://en.wikipedia.org/wiki/Joseph_Stalin

Two World Wars

We are bombarded with information that the human race is evolving, yet the plain evidence runs contrary to this. We have still not managed to create a living cell, which makes life a priceless commodity; yet we engage in acts of self-destruction beyond belief, and to an extent never seen among the lower animals. The First World War resulted in the death of 17 million people with a further 20 million wounded. At the start of the war, H. G. Wells called it *The War That Will End War* in an article in *The Daily News* on 14 August, 1914. It was to be the bloodiest war in history, but the world, and Germany in particular, failed to learn any lessons from it. In no less than 21 years the Second World War had started, and this resulted in 60 million deaths—about 3.5% of the world's population.

WE HAVE STILL NOT MANAGED TO CREATE A LIVING CELL, WHICH MAKES LIFE A PRICELESS COMMODITY; YET WE ENGAGE IN ACTS OF SELF-DESTRUCTION BEYOND BELIEF, AND TO AN EXTENT NEVER SEEN AMONG THE LOWER ANIMALS.

The motivation for wars can vary, but usually a greed for domination, power and territory, mixed with personal pride, is at the root of it. These are matters which are addressed by the Bible, with God-given laws to help regulate society and prevent such manmade catastrophes occurring.

Some are claiming that religion is a major cause of war, but recent research has shown that it has played a part in only about 7% of all wars.[21] Half of that figure is attributed to Islamic wars, and the balance to other faiths combined. It should be also noted that those who might have gone to war under a Christian banner are going counter to Christ's teaching, who said to Pilate, 'My kingdom is not of this world. If my kingdom were of this world, my servants would have been fighting, that I might not be delivered over to the Jews. But my kingdom is not from the world' (John 18:36). Jesus also said that we should love our enemies. On the occasion of his arrest in Gethsemane, Jesus warned Peter to put away his sword, because those who live by the sword will die by the sword (Matthew 26:52). In his earlier sermon on the mount, Jesus told the people that those who are blessed and happy in the world are the peacemakers (Matthew 5:9). That is not to say that we should not act in self-defence to protect our families from unlawful aggression.

THE MOTIVATION FOR WARS CAN VARY, BUT
USUALLY A GREED FOR DOMINATION, POWER
AND TERRITORY, MIXED WITH PERSONAL PRIDE,
IS AT THE ROOT OF IT.

---

[21] https://carm.org/religion-cause-war

Since the mid-1960s

The Vietnam War
The protracted and messy Vietnam War finally ended in 1975 after the withdrawal of the United States, which had seen the deaths of 58,200 of its servicemen, and from 1 to 3 million Vietnamese.

The Cambodian Genocide
In the Cambodian Genocide (1975–1979) carried out by the Khmer Rouge under their leader Pol Pot, who had adopted the ideals of Stalin and Mao, there were about 2 million deaths. About 20,000 mass graves have been discovered, which have since become known as the Killing Fields.

The Rwandan Genocide
The tribal conflict of the Rwandan Genocide (1994) between the Hutus and Tutsis resulted in from 500,000 to 1 million deaths — about 20% of the population.

Syrian Civil War
The ongoing conflict in Syria has seen the deaths of from 250,000 to 470,000 rebels, plus unknown numbers of government forces. As of February 2016, about 14 million Syrians have fled their homes, of which about 6 million have fled the country. The population in 2011 was about 23 million, which means over a quarter of the population is in exile.[22]

---

[22] https://en.wikipedia.org/wiki/Refugees_of_the_Syrian_Civil_War; and

What a piece of work is man! (*Hamlet*, Act 2, Scene 2)
Professor Brian Cox acknowledges that 'The human brain is the most complex physical structure we know of anywhere in the universe. There are around 85 billion neurons in the average human brain—that's comparable to the number of stars in the average galaxy ... Each neuron has 10,000 to 100,000 connections to other neurons.'[23]

There is no way that such a vast and complicated 'machine' could have evolved by chance, no matter how long a period of time is involved. There is more chance of a pristine Aston Martin DB11 supercar being created by bulldozing a heap of scrap cars around, or of a statue of King David being formed by an explosive blast at the Carrara marble quarries, than there is of creating a human brain by random mutations. And when you think that a brain is contained within a protective shell and needs a body with a heart to pump oxygen-containing blood around it through suitably positioned blood vessels, and for that process to function it needs a constantly pulsating lung to absorb the oxygen from the air, we have to conclude that natural forces alone are insufficient to account for human life.

---

https://en.wikipedia.org/wiki/Women_in_Syria
[23] Brian Cox and Andrew Cohen, Human Universe, William Collins, London, 2014, p. 142

3: Life

The Bible shows us that human life involved a miraculous intervention by God to initiate it, and that he continues to be active in creating every new baby to be born on planet Earth. The creation of the first person, Adam, is recorded in Genesis 2:7: 'Then the LORD God formed the man of dust from the ground and breathed into his nostrils the breath of life, and the man became a living creature.'

THERE ARE AROUND 85 BILLION NEURONS IN THE AVERAGE HUMAN BRAIN—THAT'S COMPARABLE TO THE NUMBER OF STARS IN THE AVERAGE GALAXY.

King David, writing about 1000–975 BC, recognised how God was aware and actively involved in his formation into a baby: 'For you formed my inward parts; you knitted me together in my mother's womb. I praise you, for I am fearfully and wonderfully made. Wonderful are your works; my soul knows it very well. My frame was not hidden from you when I was being made in secret, intricately woven in the depths of the earth' (Psalm 139:13–15). If anything is 'intricately woven', the system of nerves in the human brain exceeds anything else in the universe.

The prophet Jeremiah records God's word to him in about 629 BC at the commencement of his ministry: 'Before I formed you in the womb I knew you, and before you were born I consecrated you; I appointed you a prophet to the nations' (Jeremiah 1:5).

Birth of Jesus

God revealed the future birth of his Son to Isaiah, who prophesied around 730–690 BC. Isaiah records God's words to King Ahaz: 'Behold, the virgin shall conceive and bear a son, and shall call his name Immanuel' (Isaiah 7:14b). In chapter 9, verses 6 and 7, the Lord revealed more of the other names of Christ and of his eternal rule and government.

Seven hundred years later the angel Gabriel came to the Virgin Mary and announced: 'Behold, you will conceive in your womb and bear a son, and you shall call his name Jesus.' Mary, knowing she was a chaste virgin, was puzzled how this could happen. Gabriel replied: 'The Holy Spirit will come upon you, and the power of the most high will overshadow you; therefore the child to be born will be called holy—the Son of God' (Luke 1:26–35). Joseph, who was betrothed to Mary, had doubts about his forthcoming marriage, and so an angel also assured him, 'Do not fear to take Mary as your wife, for that which is conceived in her is from the Holy Spirit. She will bear a son, and you shall call his name Jesus, for he will save his people from their sins' (Matthew 1:20b–21).

God knew us, too

The apostle Paul told the gathering of believers at Ephesus, ordinary people and no doubt including slaves, 'He chose us in him before the foundation of the world, that we should be holy and blameless before him' (Ephesians 1:4). God was telling them that they were special, and that he had a purpose for them—to live lives that reflected his own character. In the beginning God 'created man in his own image' (Genesis 1:27), but man had sinned and an evil shadow had obscured the beauty of God as seen in man. Christ had come to restore that original purity and godlikeness. That possibility is open to all who come to God by trusting in Jesus, which means Saviour. Jesus said, ' … whoever comes to me I will never cast out' (John 6:37b).

> IN THE BEGINNING GOD 'CREATED MAN IN HIS OWN IMAGE' (GENESIS 1:27), BUT MAN HAD SINNED AND AN EVIL SHADOW HAD OBSCURED THE BEAUTY OF GOD AS SEEN IN MAN.

Chemical evolution

Cox and others who leave God out of their reckoning concerning origins have no other alternative than to fall back on the groundless conception that life somehow began by mixing a few chemicals together. He writes: 'It is possible that life emerged more than once on Earth, with different biochemistry, but we have no evidence of it.' So, honestly admitting he lacks any substantiating evidence, he carries on speculating that this life 'may not even have been cellular in nature, but rather a collection of biochemical reactions involving proteins and self-replicating molecules, possibly contained inside rocky chambers around deep-sea hydrothermal vents.'[24]

COX AND OTHERS WHO LEAVE GOD OUT OF THEIR RECKONING CONCERNING ORIGINS HAVE NO OTHER ALTERNATIVE THAN TO FALL BACK ON THE GROUNDLESS CONCEPTION THAT LIFE SOMEHOW BEGAN BY MIXING A FEW CHEMICALS TOGETHER.

Proteins

The chemical evolutionist argues that since we are here, we must have somehow evolved from those inorganic substances present

---

[24] Cox & Cohen, *ibid*, p. 106

3: Life

on the Earth at the time it was formed. They can only guess at the composition of the atmosphere and the possibility of lightning storms. Using carefully controlled laboratory conditions it has been possible to make some amino acids from simple inorganic substances. Obviously they would have been protected from decomposition and immediate dilution by a hostile primeval environment.

Amino acids can be left- or right-handed, with exactly the same chemical properties, and equal amounts of both are produced when synthesized from inorganic substances. Living cells only use the left-handed form in their proteins. It is impossible to conceive how any factors could exist to differentiate between these two forms of amino acid, enabling their selection to form proteins. Also, only 20 amino acids are used in living cells, yet there would be a vast number of different amino acids in any primeval soup. The simplest protein will need at least 50 amino acid residues in a specific sequence, the primary structure. These will form themselves into alpha-helixes and beta-pleated sheets as its secondary structure, and the whole chain will then fold up into the tertiary structure, the precise shape needed to allow an incoming molecule to attach itself so that it can undergo a specific reaction. White has calculated that the odds against the chance formation of a simple protein molecule containing 100 amino acids are 10^{71} against, and take 10^{80} years to form in the primeval soup.[25]

---

[25] A. J. Monty White, *What about origins?*, Dunestone Printers Ltd., 1978, p. 79

DNA

DNA is essential for the replication of all known living organisms and many viruses. It consists of chains of nucleotides, which consist of the nucleobases cytosine (C), guanine (G), adenine (A), and thymine (T), together with the sugar deoxyribose and a phosphate group. These are combined to form two parallel chains running in opposite directions and wound together into a spiral helix. The DNA in the largest human chromosome, chromosome number 1, consists of approximately 220 million base pairs, where the nucleobase on one helix is bound to the correct nucleobase on the other helix. The chance of getting all these linkages in the correct sequence is virtually impossible.

THERE CLEARLY NEEDS TO BE THE INPUT OF A DESIGNER, IN THIS CASE GUSTAVE EIFFEL, TO ENABLE THE CONSTRUCTION OF HIS FAMOUS 1,000FT TOWER BUILT IN PARIS IN 1889. THIS STRUCTURE IS FAR SIMPLER THAN THAT OF DNA,

---

Let's go back to raking over the contents of our scrap metal yard again. We are looking for a metal rivet. It has to be the right metal and exactly the right shape, the correct diameter and length. It then has to be inserted into a wrought iron girder of a specified length with the correct diameter hole situated at exactly the right distance from the end. We will need 2.5 million rivets

3: Life

and 18,000 lengths of wrought iron which must all be fitted together. It is intuitively obvious that this could not happen by pure chance, even if we could assign a mathematical probability to the event. Supposing it was possible to join everything together, we would just end up with a tangled mass of girders. There clearly needs to be the input of a designer, in this case Gustave Eiffel, to enable the construction of his famous 1,000ft tower built in Paris in 1889. This structure is far simpler than that of DNA, so if we combine that fact with the unfeasibility of chance protein formation, and all the other factors that constitute a living cell, one must look elsewhere for an explanation of the origin of life on Earth.

THIS STRUCTURE IS FAR SIMPLER THAN THAT OF DNA, SO IF WE COMBINE THAT FACT WITH THE UNFEASIBILITY OF CHANCE PROTEIN FORMATION, AND ALL THE OTHER FACTORS THAT CONSTITUTE A LIVING CELL, ONE MUST LOOK ELSEWHERE FOR AN EXPLANATION OF THE ORIGIN OF LIFE ON EARTH.

Intelligent Design (ID)

Intelligent Design has been considered as an argument against evolution by random mutations, which has been used by Creationists such as Professor Stuart Burgess. One example Burgess examines is the beauty of the peacock tail with its magnificent eyes. Even Darwin noted that 'a great number of male animals ... have been rendered beautiful for beauty's sake; the most refined beauty may serve as a charm for the female, and for no other purpose; that ornament and variety is the sole object, I have myself but little doubt.'[26]

Darwin also commented regarding the aesthetic sense of the peahen that 'It is undoubtedly a marvellous fact that she should possess this almost human degree of taste.'[27]

The iridescent beauty of the tail of the peacock relies on several factors which all need to be in place at the same time to produce the effect caused by 'thin film interference.' There needs to be a flat feather barbule, and a keratin layer which has a thickness similar to the wavelength of light. The peacock's feather has a triple keratin layer of about 0.5 microns in thickness, where 1 micron is one thousandth of a millimetre. All the colours which make up one eye spot,—purple, blue, and bronze upon a green background—are not made up of pigments, but are caused by light interference resulting from variations in the thickness of the keratin layer, which change abruptly at the colour boundaries. There is no gradual change of colour. Each eye pattern is made up of thousands of individual barbules which have a single colour unless it

---

[26] Quoted by H. Cronin, *The ant and the peacock*, Cambridge University Press, Cambridge, 1991, p. 183
[27] Charles Darwin, *The Descent of Man*, John Murray, London, 1871, p. 412

3: Life

crosses a colour boundary where the thickness of the keratin will change abruptly. Each barbule segment is about 60 microns square, giving an image resolution equivalent to printing at 280 dots per inch which is adequate for modern printing processes.[28]

It is no longer the case that only Creationists appeal to design in nature to infer that a superior intelligence is responsible for the complexity of living organisms. Dr. Stephen C. Meyer obtained his Cambridge Ph. D. in 1991 with his thesis *'Of Clues and Causes: A Methodological Interpretation of Origin-of-Life Research.'* Darwin and Lyell interpreted the clues in the fossil record to account for life as we know it using the principle of applying 'causes now in operation'. Meyer, now Director of Seattle's Center for Science and Culture at the Discovery Institute, first studied the intricate nanotechnology which operates inside living cells. He is currently applying the principle that present-day knowledge about information transmission and computing technology is a 'cause now in operation' which should be applied to interpreting the clues we have concerning the origin of living things.

THESE MOLECULAR MACHINE ENGINES LOOK LIKE THEY WERE DESIGNED BY ENGINEERS, WITH MANY DISTINCT MECHANICAL PARTS (MADE OF PROTEINS), INCLUDING ROTORS, STATORS, O-RINGS, BUSHINGS, U-JOINTS AND DRIVE SHAFTS.

---

[28] Stuart Burgess, *Hallmarks of Design*, Day One, revised edition 2002, pp. 73-97

Bacterial cells

Meyer was first struck with the complexity of a 'simple' bacterial cell. He writes: 'Bacterial cells are propelled by rotary engines called flagellar motors that rotate at 100,000rpm. These molecular machine engines look like they were designed by engineers, with many distinct mechanical parts (made of proteins), including rotors, stators, O-rings, bushings, U-joints and drive shafts.' The flagellar motor 'depends on the co-ordinated function of 30 protein parts. Remove one of these proteins and the rotary motor doesn't work. It is 'irreducibly complex'. Meyer points out that 'ID is not based on religion, but on scientific discoveries and our experience of cause and effect. Unlike creationism, ID is an inference from biological data.'[29]

The information factor

When Watson and Crick uncovered the structure of DNA in 1953, they found a precise sequence of four nucleotides which carried the code for transmitting the assembly instructions for the protein molecules which the cell needs to survive. It was equivalent to the computer machine-code we use today. Meyer says that 'no theory of undirected chemical evolution has explained the origin of the digital information needed to build the first living cell. Why? There is simply too much information in the cell to be explained by chance alone.'

NO THEORY OF UNDIRECTED CHEMICAL EVOLUTION HAS EXPLAINED THE ORIGIN OF THE DIGITAL INFORMATION NEEDED TO BUILD THE FIRST LIVING CELL.

---

[29] Stephen C. Meyer, Daily Telegraph, 28.01.2006

The Cambrian 'explosion'

In the website interview promoting his latest book *Darwin's Doubt*,[30] Meyer speaks of the problem Darwin had with the Cambrian explosion, when many animals suddenly appeared in the fossil record without apparent ancestors in earlier layers of rock. All these creatures required vast amounts of information stored in their DNA, and this is 'best explained by intelligent design, rather than purely undirected evolutionary processes.' He says: 'If you don't have instructions, if you don't have information, you can't build anything in life.'

The odds stack up

Dr. Douglas D. Axe is molecular biologist and Director of the Biologic Institute in Redmond, Washington. [31] He found that for a short protein of 150 amino-acids, there are another 10^{195} possible arrangements of those amino-acids. In addition, only one correct sequence which will enable it to fold into its tertiary structure and function as normal is possible out of 10^{77} other sequences.

There are about 10^{65} atoms in our Milky Way galaxy, so there is more chance of finding a specific atom in our galaxy, than arriving at a useful protein sequence by random mutations. Living organisms require many different proteins to function correctly, so the odds against evolution are huge beyond belief.

MEYER ARGUES THAT RANDOM CHANGES TO COMPUTER CODE OR WRITTEN SCRIPT INVARIABLY CAUSE IT TO DEGRADE OR PRODUCE GIBBERISH, RATHER THAN GIVE FUNCTION OR MEANING.

---

[30] HarperOne, 2014, www.darwinsdoubt.com
[31] http://www.biologicinstitute.org/people/

When one considers that the total number of organisms which have ever existed on the Earth, assuming the evolutionary timescale of 3.5 billion years, is only 10^{40}, which means if 'evolution' has been searching for a beneficial mutation for just one protein during this period, it would still have searched only 10 trillion-trillion-trillionth of the total possibilities.

Meyer argues that random changes to computer code or written script invariably cause it to degrade or produce gibberish, rather than give function or meaning. In explaining the past, the present is the key, and as we look to 'causes in operation' today, we see that the biological information needed for living things, such as that contained in their DNA, must come from 'intelligence'. 'We come back to a "mind," not a material process. A designing intelligence has played a role in the history of life.'

'BY FAITH WE UNDERSTAND THAT THE UNIVERSE WAS CREATED BY THE WORD OF GOD.'

~ HEBREWS 11:3 ~

Meyer is not a Creationist, and tries to give purely scientific reasons for his arguments. He is not afraid to ruffle a few Darwinian feathers along the way, and some other mainstream scientists are now suggesting we are entering a post-Darwinian era. Those who believe the Bible can go one step further and state the source of this 'designing intelligence'. 'By faith we understand that the universe was created by the word of God' (Hebrews 11:3a); 'And God said, "Let the earth bring forth living creatures according to their kinds—livestock and creeping things and beasts of the earth according to their kinds." And it was so.' (Genesis 1:24). Perhaps we need to humble ourselves like Job of old and confess: 'I know that you can do all things ... Therefore I have uttered what I did not understand, things too wonderful for me, which I did not know' (Job 42:2a, 3b).

'I KNOW THAT YOU CAN DO ALL THINGS ...
THEREFORE I HAVE UTTERED WHAT I DID NOT
UNDERSTAND, THINGS TOO WONDERFUL FOR
ME, WHICH I DID NOT KNOW.'

~ JOB 42:2A, 3B ~

Micro- and macroevolution

Hospitals have become the breeding ground of MRSA—Methicillin-resistant *Staphylococcus aureus*, which can infect open wounds and be very difficult to treat with antibiotics. Bacteria occur in their millions and, if continually exposed to antibiotics, the few which are resistant to their toxicity will survive and multiply. Eventually this will lead to a colony of a new strain of the bacteria, in our example known as HA-MRSA (Healthcare Associated MRSA). This process is known as microevolution.

Evolutionists believe that an accumulation of small steps of microevolution, each occurring over relatively short periods of time will lead, after a long time interval, to the emergence of a new species (speciation) by a process of macroevolution. Creationists accept that variation can occur within a species, but that macroevolution resulting in a new 'kind' of living organism as defined in Genesis is not possible. A type of speciation within a biblical 'kind' may be possible, but not the production of a new genus. Confusion can arise because a 'kind' of animal in Genesis may not correspond to what biologists define as a species.

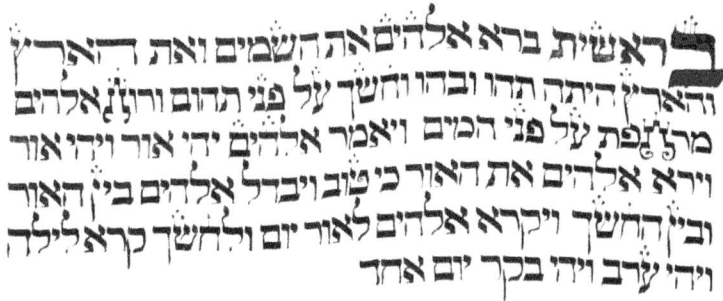

Genesis 1, the first few verses in Hebrew

Baraminology

Baraminology is the study of biblical 'kinds'. The term is derived from the Hebrew words bara, which means "to create," and min, which means "kind." This field of study shows, for example, that the many dog species that we find throughout the world today— including the coyote, the wolf, the fox, the border collie, and the jackal—may all descend from one original 'kind', created by God on Day 6 of Creation Week. Creationists may therefore envision an 'orchard' of 'kinds' rather than a single 'tree,' with variations in each 'kind' appearing as branches and twigs.[32]

---

[32] Todd C. Wood, *Two of Every Kind*, 2007, in
http://www.answersingenesis.org/articles/am/v2/n2/two-of-every-kind

Genetic variation

Even if we ignore the question of how life on earth originated, we still need to answer the question of the real effect of genetic mutations on the development of organisms. First we need a working knowledge of some of the terms involved. Eukaryotes are the type of cells found in animals, plants and yeasts. They have a nucleus which may contain multiple chromosomes. Each chromosome contains the DNA double helix which is wrapped around a structural protein molecule, called a histone, to form a chromatin. A human chromosome can have 500 million base pairs along the DNA chain. Groups of these base pairs form genes, which are the molecular units of heredity, and serve to encode the formation of functional RNA or a protein product. The gene itself may possess alternative forms, called alleles. The human somatic cell has 46 chromosomes, or 23 sets of homologous pairs. The nature of the equivalent alleles on each paired chain of DNA will determine features such as eye colour and the number of limbs.

A HUMAN CHROMOSOME CAN HAVE 500 MILLION BASE PAIRS ALONG THE DNA CHAIN. GROUPS OF THESE BASE PAIRS FORM GENES, WHICH ARE THE MOLECULAR UNITS OF HEREDITY, AND SERVE TO ENCODE THE FORMATION OF FUNCTIONAL RNA OR A PROTEIN PRODUCT.

The Blue Morpho butterfly (*Morpho Peleides Insularis*) has an iridescent blue colouration on the top (dorsal) side of its wings which reflect 70% of light, including UV light which its eyes are capable of detecting. Even a human eye can make out this butterfly at a distance of 1 km. The underside (ventral side) of the forewings and hind wings are brown, to camouflage it in the forest, and have large eyespots to intimidate and confuse predators. These features are all governed by its 28 chromosomes, with some variation within the species which will allow different numbers of eye spots.[33] [34]

Variation within a species

The domestic dog
The great variety of types of domestic dog has all been derived from a couple of ancient breeds of wild dog by careful breeding and selection over hundreds of years. The Chihuahua weighs in at about 2.2 kg and stands just 20 cm high, whereas the Newfoundland is about 70 kg and 70 cm high. There are also great variations in colour and type of hair produced by the recombination of genes, but all 'remain still within the created dog-kind that God made.'[35]

---

[33] David J. Wesley and Thomas C. Emmel, *The Chromosomes of Neotropical Butterflies from Trinidad and Tobago*, Biotropica, Vol. 7, (1), Apr. 1975, pp. 24-31

[34] Haleigh A. Ray, (Entomology and Nematology Department, University of Florida), and Jacqueline Y. Miller, (McGuire Center for Lepidoptera and Biodiversity, University of Florida), Featured Creatures—Blue Morpho Butterfly, August 2015, available at: http://entnemdept.ufl.edu/creatures/bfly/blue_morpho.htm

[35] Dr. Chris J. Pegington, *A Beginner's Guide to Creation*, Bryntirion Press, 2008, p. 31

Adaptation

If change in environmental conditions meant that the food supply of an animal became located higher up from the ground, then those with longer legs would have more chance of survival, and continue to breed selectively. This is normal adaptation and helps preserve the species during adverse conditions. Adaptation does not result in a new species. Take for instance the Mexican cave fish (*Astyanax mexicanus*), which are a blind variation of the Mexican tetra fish. Being of the same species, they are capable of interbreeding. Blind cave fish have arisen independently in several locations in the area under study, and derive from two different ancestral stocks.

It has been suggested that the eyes of fish living in total darkness would be subject to damage and infection, so those without eyes, or eyes protected by a flap of skin, would have an increased chance of survival and breeding. They navigate by sensing changes in water pressure using their lateral line organs and have become albinos, and also have taste buds under their lower jaw. [36][37][38]

These cave fish have suffered the loss or mutation of 15 to 20 genes from the hundreds needed to control eye formation. Different populations have lost different genes, so it is possible to restore sight by interbreeding.

ADAPTATION HELPS PRESERVE THE SPECIES DURING ADVERSE CONDITIONS.. ADAPTATION DOES NOT RESULT IN A NEW SPECIES.

---

[36] Brian Thomas, M.S., *Evolution Made Cavefish Go Blind?* Article in: http://www.icr.org/article/evolution-made-cavefish-go-blind

[37] J.B. Gross, *The complex origin of Astyanax cavefish".* BMC Evolutionary Biology, 12, June 2012, p. 105

[38] https://en.wikipedia.org/wiki/Mexican_tetra

3: Life

Chance mutations
Evolutionary biologists say that because body features like limbs and eyes exist, and assuming we have evolved from single-celled organisms, then they must have arisen by favourable chance mutations over a long period. We saw above that random changes to coded instructions, like that contained in DNA, invariably produces degradation of function. No new functional organ has ever been seen to arise by chance mutations, rather an impairment of the viability of the organism.

The fruit fly
Geneticists have been breeding the fruit fly, *Drosophila melanogaster*, for over a hundred years, and although about 3,000 mutations have been recorded, none have been beneficial and most have been harmful. It is worth noting that with all these mutations, scientists are still left with a fruit fly, although a rather queer one, with missing eyes or hairy backs.[39]

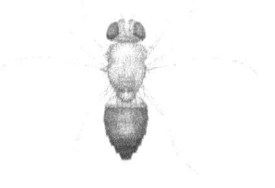

Drosophila melanogaster

Mutational build-up
Most mutations have no effect on the organism, and being too subtle to cause a difference in any trait, no process can detect them. Not even 'natural selection' is capable of detecting them, and so these subtle mutations amass relentlessly.

> Eventually, the accumulating mutations will damage vital systems and cause 'mutational meltdown,' which leads to extinction. The build-up of mutations is accelerated by small population sizes, making recovery difficult or impossible. For example, conservationists must carefully breed pandas, giant salamanders, Tasmanian devils, Bengal tigers, and many more endangered creatures with others of

---
[39] Dr. Chris J. Pegington, *ibid*, p. 32

their kinds that have the fewest mutations. But this only delays the inevitable.[40]

As for mutations in humans, in a study in the journal *Science*, it was calculated that there was a rate of 1.38×10-8 mutations per base pair per generation.[41] Given the almost 3.2 billion base pairs in the human genome, that means that each new generation accumulates 44 brand new mutations in their genes. If this process of human evolution has been going on for as long as the period suggested by evolutionists, *homo sapiens* would have been extinct long before now.

Theistic evolution

I can really understand the difficulty of studying one of the biological sciences, or of working in a college where the majority of one's colleagues accept Darwinian evolution. A student believing in the biblical account of creation cannot simply dismiss his lecture notes and present his privately studied Creationist dogma. He, or she, must be able to state the basic evolutionary facts of the taught course on which he will be marked, but is at liberty to suggest shortcomings in the theory and refer to some of the doubts which are being voiced by biologists having no Creationist agenda. The Christian will have to work extra hard in order to study and add these alternative views to learning the basic course notes.

IF THIS PROCESS OF HUMAN EVOLUTION HAS BEEN GOING ON FOR AS LONG AS THE PERIOD SUGGESTED BY EVOLUTIONISTS, HOMO SAPIENS WOULD HAVE BEEN EXTINCT LONG BEFORE NOW.

---

[40] Institute for Creation Research, http://www.icr.org/mutation-buildup/

[41] M.R. Nelson, et al., *An Abundance of Rare Functional Variants in 202 Drug Target Genes Sequenced in 14,002 People*, Science, 337 (6090), 2012, pp100-104; available from http://www.ncbi.nlm.nih.gov/pmc/articles/PMC4319976/

It is unlikely that a Christian will be happy teaching a specific course in evolutionary biology. Other aspects of biology, such as plant pathology, will only encounter evolution as a side issue. The temptation will be to try and reconcile the current evolutionary opinions, those accepted in the refereed scientific journals, with the Genesis account of creation. James Clerk Maxwell in 1876 was in correspondence with the Right Reverend C. J. Ellicott, DD, the Lord Bishop of Gloucester and Bristol, about the Genesis account of the creation of light. He expressed great caution about interpreting Scripture by the light of some new scientific discovery: 'But I should be very sorry if an interpretation founded on a most conjectural scientific hypothesis were to get fastened to the text in Genesis ... The rate of change of scientific hypothesis is naturally much more rapid than that of Biblical interpretations, so that if an interpretation is founded on such an hypothesis, it may help to keep the hypothesis above ground long after it ought to be buried and forgotten.'

Apart from that danger, there is a fundamental flaw in accepting that humans, male and female, have evolved from animals over a long period with earlier forms dying out to be replaced by more advanced creatures. One then assumes God selected one of them and breathed a special spirit of life to change him into a man in his own image. Whatever the precise mechanics of this process, there will have been the presence of death from the very beginning, which runs counter firstly to the declaration that 'God saw everything that he had made, and behold it was very good' (Genesis 1:31a).

Secondly, it is against God's curse on Adam after the Fall, that 'By the sweat of your face you will eat bread, till you return to the ground, for out of it you were taken; for you are dust, and to

3: Life

dust you shall return' (Genesis 3:19). There was no death or dying in God's physical universe until after Adam and Eve had sinned. The apostle Paul says: 'For as by a man came death, by a man has come also the resurrection of the dead. For as in Adam all die, so also in Christ shall all be made alive' (1 Corinthians 15:21–22). In verses 45 and 47 Paul says that 'The first man Adam became a living being ... The first man was from the earth, a man of dust.' So Adam was not a live humanoid animal when God selected him—he was a heap of dead dust which God formed into the most beautiful and precious being, sharing God's character and able to show love and worship to his Creator. He was someone God could have fellowship with.

Hope

The hope which God now offers mankind is a restoration to perfect purity and joy in his presence for all eternity. This can begin now because of what Jesus Christ has done in coming to planet Earth to be born, live a perfect life and then die in our place on the cross at Calvary. If we trust him, repent of our sin, and ask him into our lives, then we can really start living. This chapter has been about life, and we have to say that in addition to animal life, which is the physical life of the body, there is also a spiritual life which will continue into eternity. Jesus was sad when he said: 'yet you refuse to come to me that you may have life' (John 5:10). Later Jesus tells us why he came: 'I came that they may have life and have it abundantly' (John 10:10b).

THE HOPE WHICH GOD NOW OFFERS MANKIND
IS A RESTORATION TO PERFECT PURITY AND JOY
IN HIS PRESENCE FOR ALL ETERNITY.

Life and love

In the run-up to the United States 2016 elections, Democratic front-runner Hillary Clinton declared that America needs 'more love and kindness', which she said was preferable to 'building walls'. To protect ourselves from others and preserve ourselves from being hurt or trampled on, and to guard our acquisition of wealth and self-interest and be among the fittest that will survive, we build defensive walls about ourselves. We isolate ourselves and give others the feeling that they are outsiders and not wanted or cared for. The Christian concept of life includes an unselfish consideration of others, and follows the example of Jesus Christ who served others while on Earth, and met with lots of unfortunate people, sufferers from leprosy, prostitutes and the hated tax-collectors who collaborated with the Roman occupation.

Care for the poor

Jesus told the rich young ruler to sell his amassed goods, which had become his idol, and give the proceeds to the poor (Mark 10:17–22). The Old Testament teaching to Israel from the very beginning and enshrined in their laws was also to have compassion on the strangers or sojourners in their midst: 'You shall not wrong a sojourner or oppress him, for you were sojourners in the land of Egypt' (Exodus 22:21). Not only had they to avoid mistreating the less fortunate, they had to positively help them by being less greedy for themselves: 'When you reap the harvest of your land, you shall not reap your field right up to its edge, neither shall you gather the gleanings after your harvest. And you shall not strip your vineyard bare, neither shall you gather the fallen grapes of your vineyard. You shall leave them for the poor and for the sojourner: I am the LORD your God' (Leviticus 19:9–10).

3: Life

THE BIBLE IS THE WORKSHOP MANUAL FOR LIFE, AND GIVES GOOD ADVICE FOR THE WELFARE OF OUR POOR AND WEAK AND SICK NEIGHBOURS.

We have seen how man has left God out of the equation for life and turned his back on God's revelation, and in doing so has ended up in a very dark place. If God made man, then he knows what will make us happy and has provided us with some light on the subject. The Bible is the workshop manual for life, and gives good advice for the welfare of our poor and weak and sick neighbours. If we are all precious in God's eyes, it is not surprising that we are encouraged to help those less fortunate than ourselves; after all, who knows when we might find all our savings wiped out through no fault of our own by a crash in the stock market or an online fraudster's trick!

George Müller

The Christian alternative to 'survival of the fittest' which people hope will be themselves, is to love God, to 'love your neighbour as yourself' and, where appropriate, to 'turn the other cheek'. Throughout the centuries this attitude has resulted in the founding of hospitals, the emancipation of the slaves, the reform of our prisons and improved working conditions for factory employees, the end of child labour, and the construction of caring orphanages. Christians at the forefront of these philanthropic endeavours include William Wilberforce, Lord Shaftesbury, Elizabeth Fry, Thomas Barnardo and George Müller. The type of life envisioned by serious believers in general evolution has historically involved the denial of help and education for those considered to be retarding the onward progress of our species. Yet by God's grace that is by no means true of most evolutionists, and they retain some of the image of God in their hearts in showing compassion to their fellow beings.

4

GOD

There is far more in God than we can reduce to our logical categories.

Louis Berkhof (1873–1957) [1]

---

[1] Louis Berkhof, *Systematic Theology*, Banner of Truth, London, 1966 reprint, p445

4: God

The Bible begins: 'In the beginning, God created the heavens and the earth' (Genesis 1:1). There is no argument about it. We do not have to read long philosophical reasonings designed to prove the existence of a creator God. There is no logical argument capable of scientifically proving the existence of an infinite being to the mind of a finite being of relatively little understanding. The scientific method is useful in defining physical properties, but is just not suitable to impart even the tiniest particle of knowledge concerning the spiritual world and the role and destiny of its inhabitants.

Louis Berkhof commences his great *Systematic Theology* by stating he has 'two presuppositions, namely (1) that God exists, and (2) that He has revealed Himself in his divine Word'.[2] He noticed that some have started their theology by studying man's attempts at seeking after God, adding 'as if man ever discovered Him'.[3] He explains that 'The Christian accepts the truth of the existence of God by faith. But this faith is not a blind faith, but a faith that is based on evidence, and the evidence is found primarily in Scripture as the inspired Word of God, and secondarily in God's revelation in nature.'[4]

'THERE IS A SELF-EXISTENT, SELF-CONSCIOUS, PERSONAL BEING, WHICH IS THE ORIGIN OF ALL THINGS, AND TRANSCENDS THE ENTIRE CREATION, BUT IS AT THE SAME TIME IMMANENT IN EVERY PART OF IT.'

~ LOUIS BERKHOF ~

---

[2] Louis Berkhof, *ibid.*, p19
[3] Louis Berkhof, *ibid.*, p20
[4] Louis Berkhof, *ibid.*, p21

Theological arguments

Berkhof lists several 'rational proofs' which theologians have historically brought forward in an attempt to demonstrate the existence of God, though none is entirely satisfactory: [5]

1. *The Ontological Argument:* This was proposed by Anselm of Canterbury (1033–1109), who basically said that because we cannot imagine in the mind anything greater than God, or conceive that such a being cannot be conceived not to exist, then it must exist.[6] René Descartes (1596–1650), Gottfried Leibniz (1646–1716), and William Lane Craig (born 1949) have their own versions of this argument.
2. *The Cosmological Argument:* Everything in the world must have a cause, therefore the universe must have a cause which is indefinitely great. This was criticised by Immanuel Kant (1724–1804), who pointed out that the end result of this scheme of reasoning is that God must also have a cause.
3. *The Teleological Argument:* The existence of order, harmony, purpose and intelligence implies there is a Creator, who will also be supremely intelligent and purposeful. It reveals a great Mind, but does not necessarily prove that God exists.
4. *The Moral Argument:* This was favoured by Kant above all other arguments. There is a connection between moral behaviour and prosperity in the present life, pointing to a righteous arbiter and a Highest Good, capable of exercising a future judgement and necessitating the existence of a God to give reality to that ideal.
5. *The Historical Argument:* There has always been an awareness amongst the peoples and tribes of the world of a sense of a divine presence and the need to worship.

None of these arguments is strong enough to carry conviction in debating with atheists. They are *testimonia*, and 'important as in-

---

[5] Louis Berkhof, *ibid.*, pp26-27
[6] https://en.wikipedia.org/wiki/Ontological_argument#Anselm

terpretations of God's general revelation and as exhibiting the reasonableness of belief in a divine Being'.[7]

God is not just a philosophical concept

For Berkhof, the assumption is not that God is just a philosophical presupposition, 'but that there is a self-existent, self-conscious, personal Being, which is the origin of all things, and transcends the entire creation, but is at the same time immanent in every part of it.'[8] The being of God is, therefore, an *a priori* assumption. It is a matter of faith and belief. Could one persuade a person born without sight that the sun existed? They would feel its warmth, but could come up with other plausible explanations, suggesting various forms of energy which might cause a feeling of heat.

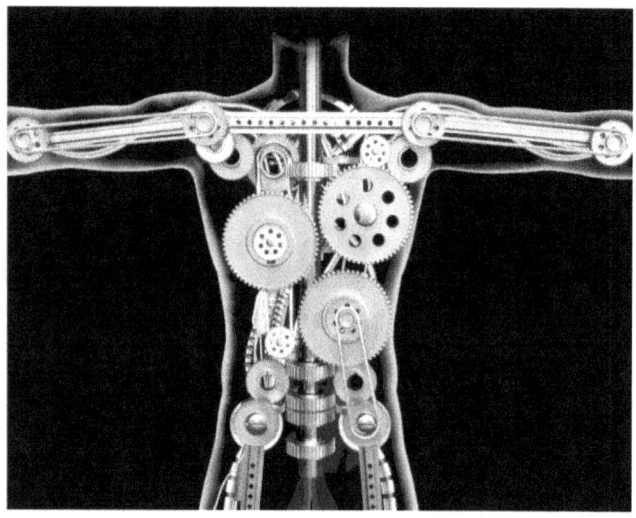

We are surrounded by evidences for God, yet we could simply deny they were anything to do with him, and carry on believing that all this ordered universe, with its laws operating in many spheres, is just a matter of chance. King David says of such a con-

---

[7] Louis Berkhof, *ibid.*, p28

[8] Louis Berkhof, *ibid.*, pp20-21

clusion: 'The fool says in his heart, "There is no God"' (Psalm 14:1a). David had looked at the heavens, the moon and stars, and was convinced that they were God's handiwork (Psalm 8:3).

Human wisdom cannot find God

The apostle Paul wrote to the sophisticated Corinthians, who lived in a major trading city about 45 miles west of Athens, hosted the Isthmian games, and had a large temple to Aphrodite: 'Where is the one who is wise? Where is the scribe? Where is the debater of this age? Has not God made foolish the wisdom of this world? For since, in the wisdom of God, the world did not know God through wisdom, it pleased God through the folly of what we preach to save those who believe' (1 Corinthians 1:20–21).

'WHERE IS THE ONE WHO IS WISE? WHERE IS THE SCRIBE? WHERE IS THE DEBATER OF THIS AGE? HAS NOT GOD MADE FOOLISH THE WISDOM OF THIS WORLD?'

~ THE APOSTLE PAUL ~

Heavenly wisdom in the New Testament

Hebrews
The author of the letter to the Hebrews begins by saying that God created the world through his Son (Hebrews 1:2). He also attributes deity to the Son, the Lord Jesus Christ, when he says, 'Your throne, O God, is forever and ever, the sceptre of uprightness is

the sceptre of your kingdom' (Hebrews 1:8, quoting Psalm 45:6). He continues, 'You, Lord, laid the foundations of the earth in the beginning, and the heavens are the work of your hands' (Hebrews 1:10).

Romans
Paul says in Romans, 'For his invisible attributes, namely, his eternal power and divine nature, have been clearly perceived, ever since the creation of the world, in the things that have been made. So they are without excuse' (Romans 1:20). Paul is arguing that an examination of the world and its creatures should clearly demonstrate to us that there is a powerful God behind everything in the universe, and who has made each of us unique.

Revelation
In his *Revelation*, the apostle John says, 'Worthy are you, our Lord and God, to receive glory and honour and power, for you created all things, and by your will they existed and were created' (Revelation 4:11).

Evidences of a Creator God

Although God's existence is not something capable of being proved, there are indicators that point to his being and power. Paul said these signs are so powerful that we are left without excuse if we deny their significance. In his book *Evidence for God*,[9] Dr. Andy Christofides has listed seven pointers to the existence of God. These are the Creation; the Coincidence that so many features of the creation have been arranged, or fine-tuned, to support life on planet Earth; the inner Craving humans have that there might be a God we can worship; our Conscience and awareness of good and evil seems unique to humans and points to a divine ori-

---

[9] Dr. Andy Christofides, *Evidence for God*, Day One, Leominster, 2010

gin; the Canon of Scripture and the way prophecies have been fulfilled, points to a divine revelation; and finally, Christ, with his miraculous birth, life, atoning death, and glorious resurrection, form part of a plan which could not have been conceived by human agencies. Andy then shows how Christian experience testifies to the truth of the life-changing power of God in our souls.

What shape is your God?

When I was a teenager I thought it would be interesting to write down what I imagined the Holy Spirit was like. The second verse of the Bible describes the Spirit of God hovering over the face of the waters. Jesus said, 'it is by the Spirit of God that I cast out demons' (Matthew 12:28). The apostle Paul says that the sons of God are led by the Spirit of God (Romans 8:14). Being naïve, I imagined that the 'of' put the Spirit in the genitive, or possessive, case, so that the Spirit was merely a property of God the Father. The Spirit was the *dunamis* (Greek), the power of God. Paul says that the risen Christ worked in him 'by the power of signs and wonders, by the power of the Spirit of God' (Romans 15:19a). I had been picking out odd texts to support my hypothesis that, in order to keep to the truth that there is only one God, the Spirit and the Son were merely God acting in power in the first instance, and taking human flesh in the second.

> 'GO THEREFORE AND MAKE DISCIPLES OF ALL NATIONS, BAPTIZING THEM IN THE NAME OF THE FATHER AND OF THE SON AND OF THE HOLY SPIRIT.'
>
> ~ THE WORDS OF JESUS ~

4: God

Although raised in a Bible-believing church, I had never grappled with the deeper teaching concerning the nature of a Trinitarian God: Father, Son and Holy Spirit. It was all a kind of fog until it was blown away when Octavius Winslow's book, *The Work of the Holy Spirit*, came into my hands.[10]

Winslow titles chapter 1, *The Godhead and Personality of the Holy Spirit*. He soon states his intention: 'In this present chapter, therefore, the distinct *personality* of the Holy Spirit will first be proved' (p. 12). He shows how the Spirit is a 'distinct intelligent agent ... in union with the Father and the Son, the one God' (p. 14).

Winslow considers the sin of blaspheming the Holy Ghost, arguing that you can only blaspheme a person, 'not an attribute, or an emanation, but a distinct person' (p. 15). The Holy Spirit is given the title of Comforter (AV), or Helper (ESV): 'he will bear witness about me' (John 15:26). Jesus also considered him a person when he said, 'If I go, I will send him to you' (John 16:7b).

Shortly before his ascension, Jesus commanded his disciples: 'Go therefore and make disciples of all nations, baptizing them in the name of the Father and of the Son and of the Holy Spirit' (Matthew 28:19). This shows that the Holy Spirit not only possesses a personal name but, being linked together in this way, must share the divine attributes of the Father and Son.[11]

The Spirit's knowledge

Another indication of distinct personality is the possession of knowledge. Paul writes: 'The Spirit himself bears witness with our spirits that we are children of God' (Romans 8:16). Paul describes to the Corinthians that the source of his spiritual wisdom is the *omniscience* of the Holy Spirit: 'these things God has revealed to us through the Spirit. For the Spirit searches everything, even the depths of God' (1 Corinthians 2:10).

David speaks of the *omnipresence* of the Spirit when he con-

---

[10] Octavius Winslow, *The Work of the Holy Spirit*, Banner of Truth, 1961; Also available from http://books.google.co.uk as *The Inquirer Directed to the Work of the Holy Spirit*, Philadelphia, Lindsay and Blakiston, 1856, 4th edn.

[11] Octavius Winslow, *ibid.*, p16

fesses: 'Where shall I go from your Spirit? Or where shall I flee from your presence? If I ascend to heaven, you are there! If I make my bed in Sheol, you are there!' (Psalm 139:7–8).

The Spirit's *omnipotence* is implied when Paul says that the signs and wonders Christ has performed through him are 'by the power of the Spirit of God' (Romans 15:18–19).

It was the Holy Spirit who sent forth the apostles (Acts 13:40. He can be grieved by corrupt talk and bad behaviour (Ephesians 4:30), and is also absolutely sovereign when he apportions spiritual gifts: 'as he wills' (1 Corinthians 12:11). The glorified Christ identifies his words with those of the Spirit when he says: 'He who has an ear, let him hear what the Spirit says to the churches' (Revelation 2:7a). Near the end of the Bible, John records that 'The Spirit and the Bride say, "Come"' (Revelation 22:17a). Here the Holy Spirit and the Bride, which is the church of God, are appealing for all who are spiritually thirsty to come and take the water of life without having to pay anything—Christ has already paid for everything by his atoning death on our behalf.

Jesus Christ—the Son of God

It has become extremely difficult to find Christmas cards having pictures of anything to do with the birth of Jesus at Bethlehem over 2,000 years ago. There are robins, snowmen, Father Christmases, and village inns blanketed in snow, but few with shepherds, wise men, or Mary and Joseph with baby Jesus in a manger. When I was a boy, most cards were 'religious' and other types with images of Santa Claus considered somewhat pagan.

It was easy to grow up assuming that when God came to Earth as the baby Jesus, this was the first time that the Son of God had

4: God

existed. It was certainly the first moment in cosmic time when he had taken human flesh in order to identify with us as a man, which would in due course enable him to live a perfect life in order to provide us with the gift of righteousness, and then suffer and die in our place, so we would not have to bear the punishment our sins deserve. This would open the way for us to possess eternal life and live with him for ever in heaven.

Christ's heavenly pre-existence

Before Christ took on the incarnate name of Jesus, as Mary was instructed by the angel Gabriel (Luke 1:31), he was eternally present with the Father in heaven as the Son of God. The apostle Paul explains this to the church at Philippi: 'Have this mind among yourselves, which is yours in Christ Jesus, who, though he was in the form of God, did not count equality with God a thing to be grasped, but emptied himself, by taking the form of a servant, being born in the likeness of men. And being found in human form, he humbled himself by becoming obedient to the point of death, even death on a cross' (Philippians 2:5–8).

IN ORDER TO LIVE AS A MAN UPON OUR PLANET JESUS HAD TO LAY ASIDE THAT GLORY IN ORDER TO BECOME NOT A POTENTATE, BUT A SERVANT.

Here we see Christ as being equal in form and essence with God the Father, but in order to live as a man upon our planet he had to lay aside that glory in order to become not a potentate, but a servant. He would serve mankind by becoming a sacrifice on their behalf, and so fulfil the meaning of his name 'Jesus', which is 'God saves'.

4: God

In 1886 the Massachusetts Baptist minister Francis H. Rowley (1854–1952) wrote the following stanza of a hymn which reflects the above truth:

> *I will sing the wondrous story*
> *Of the Christ Who died for me.*
> *How He left His home in glory*
> *For the cross of Calvary.*

We met with the late Puritan John Flavel in the chapter on Time. Christ's pre-existence in heaven was another doctrine which was unclear to me as a young believer until I read Flavel's works. In his second sermon, where he *Sets forth Christ in his essential and primeval GLORY,* he quotes Proverbs 8:30 (AV): 'Then I was by him, as one brought up with him: and I was daily his delight, rejoicing always before him...' Flavel adds that the Spirit of God, through Solomon, 'describes the most blessed state of Jesus Christ, the wisdom of the Father, from those eternal delights he had with his Father, before his assumption of our nature.'[12]

The Son of God was therefore joyfully present with the Father both before and at the time of the Creation. Indeed, 'The LORD possessed me in the beginning of his way, before his works of old' (Proverbs 8:22 AV). This loving relationship, with its co-operation and sharing, explains the verse in Genesis 1:26a: 'Then God said, "Let us make man in our image, after our likeness."' Although Genesis 1:1 (ESV) says that 'In the beginning God cre-

---

[12] John Flavel, *The Works of John Flavel*, Volume 1, Banner of Truth, London, 1968 (reprint), pp42-43; also available from archive.org as *The Whole Works of the Rev. John Flavel*, Baynes and Son, London, 1820

ated the heavens and the earth,' the apostle John explains that this work was delegated to the Son. He says, 'All things were made through him, and without him was not anything made that was made' (John 1:3). God shared his creatorship with the Son, just as he shares his divinity, so the author of *Hebrews* can write about Christ: 'He is the radiance of the glory of God and the exact imprint of his nature, and he upholds the universe by the word of his power. After making purification for sins, he sat down at the right hand of the Majesty on high ...' (Hebrews 1:3).

Michael Reeves says, 'Ultimately, the Father sent the Son because the Father so loved the Son—and wanted to share that love and fellowship. His love for the world is the overflow of his almighty love for his Son.'[13] The affectionate nature of God, shown in his love for the Son, enables him to be a truly loving God, unlike any other of the so-called gods who have a solitary or Unitarian existence, and this is the love he shares with us, and we share with others. The hymnist Anna Letitia Waring (1823–1910) could write with confidence in 1850:

In heavenly love abiding,
No change my heart shall fear;
And safe is such confiding,
For nothing changes here:
The storm may roar without me,
My heart may low be laid;
But God is round about me,
And can I be dismayed?

---

[13] Michael Reeves, *The Good God*, Paternoster, Milton Keynes, 2013 (reprint), pp51-52

Christ in prophecy

The first gospel
Immediately after the Fall of Adam and Eve, when sin and its curse of death and disease entered the world, God promised there would be a deliverer. He would be born into the world through a woman just like Eve. God said to the Devil, 'I will put enmity between you and the woman, and between your offspring and her offspring; he shall bruise your head, and you shall bruise his heel' (Genesis 3:15). This is known as the *proto-evangel*, the first gospel or good news of hope and redemption.

On Calvary, Jesus Christ fatally wounded Satan, so that he lost his power over death which had come upon man along with the whole of creation. Christ seized the keys of death and the grave, declaring, 'I died, and behold I am alive forevermore, and I have the keys of Death and Hades' (Revelation 1:18), but he had to suffer, including the wounding of his feet, in order to do so.

Christ the Star
In the progressive revelation of the Old Testament, God prophesied through Balaam that a star, the Messiah, should come out of Jacob's future family (Numbers 24:17). This was to be no ordinary man, so Isaiah prophesies that the root of Jesse, (the father of David who was Jesus' ancestor), will 'stand as a signal for the peoples—of him shall the nations inquire, and his resting place shall be glorious' (Isaiah 11:10 and Romans 15:12). Even now, according to the author of *Hebrews*, 'the point in what we are saying is this: we have such a high priest, one who is seated at the right hand of the throne of the Majesty in heaven' (Hebrews 8:1). Christ's resting place is seated with the Father in glory until he comes again to judge all peoples and restore the Creation to a perfect state.

Christ will come as a child
The Messiah was to come from the tribe of Judah and the family of Jesse, so we find he was called 'Son of David'. The first verse of

4: God

Matthew's Gospel begins with: 'The book of the genealogy of Jesus Christ, the son of David, the son of Abraham.' Isaiah again prophesied : 'For to us a child is born, to us a son is given; and the government shall be upon his shoulders, and his name shall be called Wonderful Counsellor, Mighty God, Everlasting Father, Prince of Peace (Isaiah 9:6).

ISAIAH PROPHESIED: 'FOR TO US A CHILD IS BORN, TO US A SON IS GIVEN; AND THE GOVERNMENT SHALL BE UPON HIS SHOULDERS.'

These titles can only belong to a divine ruler. The prophet Micah stated that this ruler would be born in David's ancestral home town of Bethlehem: 'But you, O Bethlehem Ephrathah, who are too little to be among the clans of Judah, from you shall come forth for me one who is to be ruler in Israel, whose coming forth is from of old, from ancient days' (Micah 5:2). This not only predicts the birth of Jesus, but reveals that his previous existence extends beyond the beginning of history. Daniel saw that 'the Ancient of Days came, and judgment was given for the saints of the Most High, and the time came when the saints possessed the kingdom' (Daniel 7:22).

Testimony to Christ in the Gospels

Mark tells us that 'Jesus came into Galilee proclaiming the gospel of God, and saying, "The time is fulfilled and the kingdom of God is at hand; repent and believe the gospel"' (Mark 1:14b–15). This was the kingdom foretold by Daniel, with Christ as supreme ruler. Although Jesus Christ came as a sacrificial Lamb to achieve our salvation, his glory was veiled and he was known as the carpenter from Nazareth (Mark 6:3). Yet in *Revelation* we read: 'They will make war on the Lamb, and the Lamb will conquer them, for he is Lord of lords and King of kings, and those with him are called and chosen and faithful' (Revelation 17:14). This is the one Isaiah said would have 'the government upon his shoulders'.

When the angel Gabriel appeared to Mary at the annunciation of her birth, he said: 'And behold, you will conceive in your womb and bear a son, and you shall call his name Jesus. He will be great and will be called the Son of the Most High. And the Lord God will give to him the throne of his father David, and he will reign over the house of Jacob forever, and of his kingdom there will be no end' (Luke 1:32–33). This left no doubt that her son was to be the prophesied Messiah.

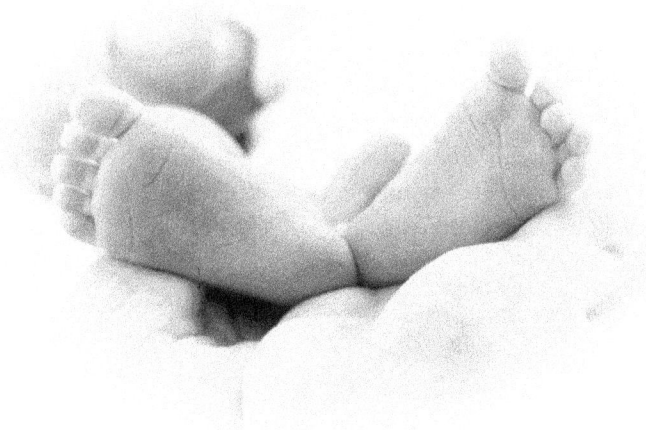

4: God

> 'YOU WILL CONCEIVE IN YOUR WOMB AND BEAR
> A SON, AND YOU SHALL CALL HIS NAME JESUS. HE
> WILL BE GREAT AND WILL BE CALLED
> THE SON OF THE MOST HIGH.'

The virgin birth

Isaiah had prophesied: 'Therefore the Lord himself will give you a sign. Behold, the virgin shall conceive and bear a son, and shall call his name Immanuel' (Isaiah 7:14). Mary was also told by the angel Gabriel that, while still remaining a virgin, 'the Spirit will come upon you, and the power of the Most High will overshadow you; therefore the child to be born will be called holy—the Son of God' (Luke 1:35). God took the tiny egg produced by Mary's ovary and by a miraculous work of the Holy Spirit, enabled it to become the Son of God in the flesh. The egg itself was not a person, and could therefore be considered morally sinless and free of guilt. The sinless Son of God came from heaven and took this sinless flesh upon himself. He could therefore fulfil the role of being the 'lamb without blemish or spot' (1 Peter 1:19), in fulfilment of the command: 'Your lamb shall be without blemish, a male a year old' (Exodus 12:5a). In this way Jesus became a perfect man, and so could represent men and women as an acceptable sacrifice before God on their behalf. He was also fully God, so his sacrifice could have infinite merit and worth, and be valid for the deliverance of all who put their trust in him.

4: God

The *Heidelberg Catechism* of 1563, questions 16 and 17, summarises the reasons for the humanity and deity of Christ:[14]

> Q 16. Why must he be a true and righteous man?
> A. He must be a true man because the justice of God requires that the same human nature which has sinned should pay for sin.¹
> He must be a righteous man because one who himself is a sinner cannot pay for others.²
> 1. Romans 5:12, 15; 1 Corinthians 15:21; Hebrews 2:14–16.
> 2. Hebrews 7:26, 27; 1 Peter 3:18.
> Q 17. Why must he at the same time be true God?
> A. He must be true God so that by the power of his divine nature ⁽¹⁾ he might bear in his human nature the burden of God's wrath,⁽²⁾ and might obtain for us and restore to us righteousness and life.⁽³⁾
> 1. Isaiah 9:6.
> 2. Deuteronomy 4:24; Nahum 1:6; Psalm 130:3.
> 3. Isaiah 53:5, 11; John 3:16; 2 Corinthians 5:21

Heidelberg Castle

---

[14] http://heidelberg-catechism.com/pdf/lords-days/Heidelberg-Catechism.pdf

4: God

The creed of Athanasius (AD 293–373) spells out these truths unequivocally in order to defend orthodoxy from the attacks of Arianism, a belief system that considered Jesus not to be completely divine. The relevant section is given below:

But it is necessary for eternal salvation that one also believe in the incarnation of our Lord Jesus Christ faithfully.

Now this is the true faith:

That we believe and confess that our Lord Jesus Christ, God's Son, is both God and human, equally.

He is God from the essence of the Father, begotten before time; and he is human from the essence of his mother, born in time; completely God, completely human, with a rational soul and human flesh; equal to the Father as regards divinity, less than the Father as regards humanity.

Although he is God and human, yet Christ is not two, but one.
He is one, however, not by his divinity being turned into flesh, but by God's taking humanity to himself.
He is one, certainly not by the blending of his essence, but by the unity of his person.
For just as one human is both rational soul and flesh, so too the one Christ is both God and human.[15]

---

[15] © 1987, CRC Publications, Grand Rapids MI. www.crcna.org. Reprinted with permission

Just after the birth of Jesus, Luke speaks of the angel who proclaimed to the shepherds near Bethlehem that 'unto you is born this day in the city of David a Saviour who is Christ the Lord' (Luke 2:11). The long-ago-promised Messiah has come at last!

> GOD WAS REACHING DOWN TO REVEAL TO
> HUMANITY HIS VERY NATURE, SO THAT WE
> WOULD KNOW FAR MORE ABOUT HIM,
> OURSELVES AND THE MEANING OF
> THE UNIVERSE AND LIFE.

John's concept of Christ as the Word

The apostle John begins his Gospel with the life-transforming thought that his beloved Saviour is the Word of God by which God the Father has been pleased to communicate his love to the world. God was reaching down to reveal to humanity his very nature, so that we would know far more about him, ourselves and the meaning of the universe and life—especially eternal life and the way to heaven. If we understand something about Jesus Christ, we will know something about God. Jesus said, 'If you had known me, you would have known my Father also. From now on you do know him and have seen him' (John 14:7). John tells us: 'In the beginning was the Word, and the Word was with God, and the Word was God. He was in the beginning with God. All things were made through him, and without him was not any thing made that was made (John 1:1–3).

The powerful Word

John is telling us that this Word was not just a philosophical proposition, a mere idea about a divine person, but was a Word imbued with creative power, with whom all things are possible.

4: God

This power also accompanies the true preaching of the gospel of God which is faithful to the Scriptures. Paul told the church at Thessalonica: 'Our gospel came to you not only in word, but also in power and in the Holy Spirit and with full conviction' (1 Thessalonians 1:5a).

John begins his first letter with the intention that we might be convinced that Jesus Christ really existed, and that it is through both the Word, and by believing his words, that we will obtain eternal life: 'That which was from the beginning, which we have heard, which we have seen with our eyes, which we looked upon and have touched with our hands, concerning the word of life — the life was made manifest, and we have seen it, and testify to it and proclaim to you the eternal life, which was with the Father and was made manifest to us—' (1 John 1:1–2).

The hymn writer Josiah Conder (1789–1855) was captured by the thought of Christ as the divine Word when he wrote:

Thou art the everlasting Word,
The Father's only Son;
God manifestly seen and heard,
And Heav'n's belovèd one:

Worthy, O Lamb of God, art Thou
That every knee to Thee should bow.

In Thee most perfectly expressed
The Father's glories shine;
Of the full deity possessed,
Eternally divine:

Worthy, O Lamb of God, art Thou
That every knee to Thee should bow.

The Trinity

If, as John tells us, Jesus Christ made all things, then he himself could not have been made. As we saw when considering *Christ's heavenly pre-existence,* Christ must be divine and so, along with the Father and the Holy Spirit, be a member of the Godhead of the three persons which constitute the One God, for which the theological term is the Trinity. Although this term is not found in the Bible, it is the inescapable truth that there are three persons in the Godhead. We exist as individual persons, but God exists as three persons in perfect harmony and agreement within the unity of God.

THERE ARE THREE PERSONS IN THE GODHEAD. WE EXIST AS INDIVIDUAL PERSONS, BUT GOD EXISTS AS THREE PERSONS IN PERFECT HARMONY AND AGREEMENT WITHIN THE UNITY OF GOD.

The Shield of the Trinity symbol, where God is represented as being tri-personal — but not a fourth entity at the centre.

Testimony about Christ in *Hebrews*

The author of *Hebrews* wrote about Christ: 'He is the radiance of the glory of God and the exact imprint of his nature, and he upholds the universe by the word of his power. After making purification for sins, he sat down at the right hand of the Majesty on high …' (Hebrews 1:3). The Lord Jesus Christ, having completed his earthly work ('When Jesus had received the sour wine, he said, "It is finished," and he bowed his head and gave up his spirit' — John 19:30), is now seated on God's throne — implying he is equal in every one of his attributes to the Father, though each person in the Trinity has a special role to play in what is known as the 'divine economy'. (For a convincing and 'accessible' treatment of the Trinity, and the wonderful interaction between the persons of the Godhead, refer to Michael Reeves' book, *The Good God*, mentioned earlier, reference 13.)

Fact not fiction

The miraculous events of the birth and resurrection of Christ may sound like mythology, but they are rooted in history. Luke was writing his Gospel to convince a somewhat sceptical Theophilus, and was careful to back up his account with facts which could be checked out for accuracy. He interviewed eyewitnesses to make sure the stories he was told were accurate: 'Inasmuch as many have undertaken to compile a narrative of the things that have been accomplished among us, just as those who from the beginning were eyewitnesses and ministers of the word have delivered them to us, it seemed good to me also, having followed all things closely for some time past, to write an orderly account for you, most excellent Theophilus, that you may have certainty concerning the things you have been taught' (Luke 1:1–4).

Luke begins his narrative with a name known to all the local people, King Herod: 'In the days of Herod, king of Judah, there was a priest named Zechariah...' (Luke 1:5a). The account of Jesus' death mentions that another ruler, Pilate, brought Jesus to Herod, who was in Jerusalem at that time (Luke 23:6–7). Luke adds that although these two had been enemies, they became friends from this day (Luke 23:12). These are the sort of details only available from those who witnessed these events.

Witnesses to the resurrected Christ

Luke records the names of those who saw the empty tomb: Mary Magdalene, Joanna, and Mary the mother of James (Luke 24:10); also the sceptical Peter, who ran to the tomb and returned home marvelling at what had happened (Luke 24:12b). Shortly afterwards, the Lord appeared to Simon Peter (Luke 24:34), and to Cleopas and another disciple walking on the road to Emmaus (Luke 24:13–32).

THERE ARE SEVERAL ACCOUNTS ABOUT THE EXISTENCE OF JESUS CHRIST FROM HISTORIANS WHO HAD NO REASON TO PROMOTE THE CAUSE OF CHRISTIANITY.

Paul says the risen Christ also 'appeared to more than five hundred brothers at one time, most of whom are still alive, though some have fallen asleep' (1 Corinthians 15:6). He was obviously writing when many eyewitnesses of the resurrected Christ were still alive. These people, or their unbelieving contemporaries, would have objected to any falsification of the facts, but the apostolic records still stand intact after nearly 2,000 years.

Testimony from secular historians

There are several accounts about the existence of Jesus Christ from historians who had no reason to promote the cause of Christianity, but were distanced from it.

Josephus
The most well-known of these is Titus Flavius Josephus (c. AD 37–100). He began as a Pharisaical Jew, and ended as a Roman citizen,

4: God

an interpreter for the Emperor when he invaded Jerusalem, and military historian. He referred to Jesus Christ in his work *The Antiquities of the Jews*. In book 18, chapter 3.3 he wrote:

> Now there was about this time Jesus, a wise man, if it be lawful to call him a man; for he was a doer of wonderful works, a teacher of such men as receive the truth with pleasure ... He was the Christ. And when Pilate, at the suggestion of the principal men amongst us, had condemned him to the cross, those that loved him did not forsake him; for he appeared to them alive again the third day; as the divine prophets had foretold these and ten thousand other wonderful things concerning him. And the tribe of Christians, so named from him, are not extinct at this day.

Josephus

Tacitus

Less well-known, but considered the greatest Roman historian, is Publius Cornelius Tacitus (c. AD 56–117). He wrote the *Annals* and *Histories* of the Roman emperors. The *Annals* is one of the earliest secular histories to mention Christ, which he does in connection with Nero's persecution of the Christians.

> Christus, from whom the name [Christians] had its origin, suffered the extreme penalty during the reign of Tiberius at the hands of one of our procurators, Pontius Pilate ...[16]

Suetonius
Gaius Suetonius Tranquillus (c. AD 69–122) wrote a set of biographies of twelve successive Roman rulers, from Julius Caesar to Domitian.[17]

In his life of Tiberius Claudius Drusus Caesar, chapter 25.4, he reports: 'He banished from Rome all the Jews, who were continually making disturbances at the instigation of one Chrestus.' ('Chrestus' is the way Suetonius spelt Christus—Christ.) This ties in with the account of how the two believers Aquila and Priscilla were expelled from Rome: 'And he [Paul] found a Jew named Aquila, a native of Pontus, recently come from Italy with his wife Priscilla, because Claudius had commanded all the Jews to leave Rome. And he went to see them, and because he was of the same trade he stayed with them and worked, for they were tentmakers by trade' (Acts 18:2–3).

Tallus
Tallus, wrote a history of the Eastern Mediterranean in about AD 52, and is quoted by Julius Africanus in about AD 221. He quotes Tallus' comments about the darkness that covered the land during the late-afternoon hours when Jesus died on the cross. Julius wrote: 'Tallus, in the third book of his histories, explains away this darkness as an eclipse of the sun unreasonably, as it seems to me' (unreasonably of course, because a solar eclipse could not take place at the time of the full moon, and it was at the season of the

---

[16] Publius Cornelius Tacitus, *Annals*, Book XV, chapter 44
[17] G. Suetonius Tranquillus, *The Lives of the Twelve Caesars*, (available from http://www.gutenberg.org/ebooks/6400).

4: God

Paschal full moon that Christ died).[18] This implies that people were well aware that there was an unusual darkness at the time of Christ's crucifixion, and it had become a matter for debate and speculation as to its cause.

Historians agree that the evidence favours the fact that there really was a person called Jesus Christ. They tend, however, to dismiss any reference to the miraculous, claiming the manuscripts have been subsequently amended by those holding Christian beliefs. That opinion may simply be a reflection of their prejudice against such a possibility. At the end of the day, we have to get the most reliable documents and see how they fit in with the unity of the body of Scripture.

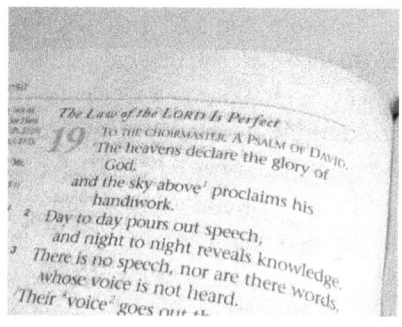

The Bible

The Bible is a collection of 66 books: 39 in the Old Testament and 27 in the New Testament. Expert scholars and theologians, skilled in the original languages, have done the groundwork for us, and collated them into its present format. Revisions have been made following the discovery of more historic documents, but these have been minor corrections and have not affected the basic teaching of the historic apostolic faith. The most well-known version has been the King James I Authorised Version of 1611 (the AV or KJV). This was achieved by a group of 47 scholars who translated the Old Testament from Hebrew and Aramaic, and the New Tes-

---

[18] Julius Africanus, *Chronography*, 18.1; see: *The Oldest Secular Accounts & Historical Evidence on the Existence of Jesus of Nazareth*, agapebiblestudy.com

tament from the Greek. Some of the rather quaint language has been updated in the more recent New King James Version (1982). The English Standard Version (revised 2011), is a modern literal translation but in the general style of the AV. The New International Version (NIV) is also very popular, and is an original translation by a group of over 100 scholars; it was updated in 2011. One must be careful in choosing a modern version to get either the anglicised edition for UK English or the American English version.

THE OLD TESTAMENT IS NEEDED TODAY TO SHOW US WHY CHRIST WAS TO COME, AND HOW HE WOULD COME; THE NEW TESTAMENT SHOWS US THAT HE DID COME AS SON OF MAN AND SON OF GOD.

Jesus' use of the Scriptures

It is worth noting that Jesus quoted from 24 out of the 39 books of the Old Testament. After the resurrection, while with his disciples, Jesus 'said to them, "These are my words that I spoke to you while I was still with you, that everything written about me in the Law of Moses and the Prophets and the Psalms must be fulfilled"' (Luke 24:44). The Old Testament is needed today to show us why Christ was to come, and how he would come; the New Testament shows us that he did come as Son of Man and Son of God, and the manner in which he is choosing and saving a people, the church, to be his heavenly Bride.

The letters written by Paul

The apostle Peter also considered that the letters of Paul were to be considered as scriptural: 'And count the patience of our Lord as salvation, just as our beloved brother Paul also wrote to you according to the wisdom given him, as he does in all his letters when he speaks in them of these matters. There are some things in them that are hard to understand, which the ignorant and unstable twist to their own destruction, as they do the other Scriptures' (2 Peter 3:15–16).

The Truth

The Lord Jesus Christ said, 'I am the way, and the truth, and the life. No one comes to the Father except through me' (John 14:6). God is very concerned that we should know the truth, and is himself the embodiment of truth. He has protected the record of the truth in the Scriptures by the inspiration of the Holy Spirit. They are even described as being 'breathed out' by the Holy Spirit: 'All Scripture is breathed out by God and profitable for teaching, for reproof, for correction, and for training in righteousness, that the man of God may be complete, equipped for every good work (2 Timothy 3:16–17). A few years ago, after about 45 years of his preaching ministry, I was present when Dr. Geoff Thomas of Aberystwyth was speaking about his belief in the Christian gospel. He said, 'If someone were to ask me why I believed it, my answer would be "Because it is true."' He could have given a lecture on all the arguments we have briefly touched on but, in the final analysis, all our reasons boil down to the simplest phrase of just four words, 'because it is true'. It claims to be true, it is historically true, and experience shows it to be true.

> GOD IS VERY CONCERNED THAT WE SHOULD KNOW THE TRUTH, AND IS HIMSELF THE EMBODIMENT OF TRUTH. HE HAS PROTECTED THE RECORD OF THE TRUTH IN THE SCRIPTURES BY THE INSPIRATION OF THE HOLY SPIRIT.

The noble army of martyrs

The Scriptures have stood the test of time and believers through the ages have found its promises to be true. This has been especially the case with those who have been martyred for their faith. The *Book of Common Prayer* contains the hymn of Ambrose, the *Te Deum*, which includes the line: 'The noble army of Martyrs : praise thee.' Paul would soon be such a martyr when he wrote: 'as it is my eager expectation and hope that I will not be at all ashamed, but that with full courage now as always Christ will be honoured in my body, whether by life or by death. For to me to live is Christ, and to die is gain' (Philippians 1:20–21). He had the assurance that he would be alive in glory with the Lord after his earthly death: 'I am hard pressed between the two. My desire is to depart and be with Christ, for that is far better' (Philippians 1:23). The martyrs have a special mention in *Revelation* when we see them under the altar in heaven: 'When he opened the fifth seal, I saw under the altar the souls of those who had been slain for the word of God and for the witness they had borne (Revelation 6:9).

William Tyndale

William Tyndale

William Tyndale (c. 1494–1536) spent much of his life translating the Bible into English to make it available to everyone, and not just those scholars and theologians who could read the Latin version. He translated painstakingly from the original languages of Hebrew and Greek to try and achieve the highest accuracy. It was strictly against the law, so he fled to Europe to continue his labours. Eventually he was betrayed, arrested, strangled and burned at the stake. His final words were, 'Lord, open the King of England's eyes!' Within just four years, Henry VIII had authorised the publication of the English Bible, including his official Great Bible in 1539. The clergy were told it was to be 'set up in some convenient place within the said church … where your parishioners may most commodiously resort to read it'.[19]

Hugh Latimer

Hugh Latimer (c. 1487–1555), Bishop of Worcester, was burned alive at the stake outside Balliol College, Oxford, by the order of Queen Mary I, known as 'Bloody Mary', because of his biblical beliefs and a refusal to acknowledge the Roman Catholic doctrine of transubstantiation—that the bread and wine at the communion service are changed into the actual body and blood of Christ. His companion at the stake was Nicholas Ridley (c. 1500–1555), Bishop of London and Westminster, to whom he addressed these famous words as a burning faggot was placed at Ridley's feet:

> Be of good comfort, Brother Ridley, and play the man; we shall this day light such a candle, by God's grace, in England, as I trust never shall be put out.[20]

These words from the stake were responsible for my own spiritual awakening, proving that God can sometimes answer prayers over 400 years into the future.

---

[19] https://en.wikipedia.org/wiki/Great_Bible

[20] Quoted in J. C. Ryle, *Five English Reformers*, Banner of Truth, London, 1960, p109

Hugh Latimer

Epilogue

The martyrs mentioned in the previous pages, along with Archbishop Cranmer (1489–1556) and John Bradford (1510–1555), once Chaplain to Edward VI, were imprisoned in the Tower of London prior to their execution. According to Latimer they 'did together read over the New Testament with great deliberation and painful study' and could find no trace of transubstantiation in it. We can be quite sure that they utterly trusted the text of their Bibles, as their very lives depended on it. The same reliance on the truth of the Scriptures can be assumed for all the Christian martyrs down the ages, including the horrific killings and beheadings in this twenty-first century.

The Tower of London today

This book has been an attempt to keep that gospel light shining in an age when the darkness of ignorance and superstition is again threatening to obscure so much of the truth for which our believing ancestors have sacrificed their lives. They had a sure conviction of life after death, and that the only way to obtain it is through the One who said he was the Way. My prayer is that you will find that Way, and a good starting point is to read the Bible, perhaps starting with the Gospel of Mark, and also seek out a church which believes the Bible to be God's Word and preaches faithfully from it.

To readers who are already believers in Christ, we need to be aware that it is all too easy just to accumulate knowledge about our faith, and fall short on experiencing the assurance, comfort and joy it can bring, and the love, without which all knowledge is empty vanity. Paul realised this when he said: 'And if I have prophetic powers, and understand all mysteries and all knowledge, and if I have all faith, so as to remove mountains, but have not love, I am nothing' (1 Corinthians 13:2). Our religion must be not only known, but also felt, as the hymnist Joseph Hart (1712–1768) realised when he wrote:

> *Let us ask the important question;*
> *(Brethren, be not too secure,)*
> *What it is to be a Christian;*
> *How we may our hearts assure.*
> *Vain is all our best devotion,*
> *If on false foundation built;*
> *True religion's more than notion —*
> *Something must be known and felt."*[21]

---

[21] http://beholdyourgod.org/2015/06/let-us-ask-the-important-question/

Bibliography for Chapter 1

J. Tyndall, *Faraday as a Discoverer*, 5th Edition, 1893 [http://www.gutenberg.org/cache/epub/1225/pg1225.txt].

Isaac Watts, *The improvement of the Mind*, New Brunswick, 1813 [https://archive.org/details/improvementofmin00].

Wikipedia: https://en.wikipedia.org/wiki/Michael_Faraday
Ian Hutchinson, *James Clerk Maxwell and the Christian Proposition*, MIT IAP Seminar: *The Faith of Great Scientists*, Jan 1998, from http://silas.psfc.mit.edu/Maxwell/maxwell.html

Illustration Credits

Illustrations for this book have been obtained from the following sources and are generally in the public domain and/or used with permission. Special mention is made of the following:

www.AnswersInGenesis.org
101

Author
21 (upper), 22, 38 (upper), 40, 53, 70, 86, 116, 118, 123, 129, 153, 169, 172, 173, 183, 198, 205

www.DepositPhotos.com
146, 149, 150, 155, 156, 159, 163, 176, 177

www.NASA.gov
47, 87, 90, 120

www.PublicDomainImages.com
8, 19, 21, 34, 37, 51, 83, 95, 96, 100, 111, 115, 126, 145, 147, 149, 167, 178, 186, 187

Wikipedia/Wikimedia Commons
20, 23, 24, 25, 27, 30, 35, 38, 42, 44, 45, 47, 55, 59, 61, 64, 67, 69, 70 (upper), 71, 72, 73, 74, 75, 78, 79, 81, 84, 92, 98, 102, 103, 109, 112, 119, 125, 127, 128, 130, 132, 133, 135 (both), 138, 139, 140, 142, 143, 144, 170, 188, 189, 196, 201, 203, 204

Other Public Domain Sources
66, 151, 152, 165

About the Author

Born in Bristol (UK), Nigel Faithfull went to Aberystwyth (Wales) in 1965 as a Christian, aged twenty-two, to read Chemistry. He graduated in Chemistry (BSc & MSc) and obtained a PhD in Analytical Chemistry in 1976. In 1970 he married Eileen, a graduate in Welsh, and was President of the Christian Union from 1970-71. Nigel continued in employment at the university, becoming Senior Research Associate in the field of agricultural analytical chemistry.

Taking early retirement in 2000, he wrote a handbook on his subject entitled *Methods in Agricultural Chemical Analysis*, published in 2002, and still being cited worldwide today. Since moving in 2010 to Newport (South Wales) to be nearer their family of two children and four grandchildren, Nigel and Eileen have been worshipping at St Mellons Baptist Church, Cardiff, where Dr. Andy Christofides is the pastor.

Nigel's hobbies include photography, cryptic crosswords, woodturning, writing articles on Christian subjects, and amusing the grandchildren. He is the author of *Thoughts Fixed and Affections Flaming*, (DayOne, 2012) and edited *Words of Encouragement*, (DayOne, 2015).

Select Index

Abraham 186
Adam 94-95, 103, 108, 126, 148, 167-168, 185
Africanus, Julius .... 197-198 +ref.
Ahaz, King 149
Albert, Prince 44
Ambrose 201
Anaximander of Miletus 125-126
Aquila 197
Aquinas, Thomas 130
Aristotle 33, 127, 128, 130, 136
Athanasius 190
Augustine, Saint 59, 63, 72, 113, 114, 130
Axe, Dr. Douglas D. 158
Baden Powell, Robert .... 135-136 + ref.
Barnardo, Thomas 171
Berkhof, Louis 72 + ref., 73, 106 + ref., 173 + ref., 174 + refs., 175-6 + refs.
Blanchard, John .... 82 ref.
Bradford, John 204
Brentnall, John M. .... 135 ref.
Bukharin, Nikolai 142
Burgess, Professor Stuart .... 154, 156 ref.
Caesar, Julius 197
Calvin, John & Calvinist 78, 81, 82, 131
Campbell, Lewis .... 47 & 57 refs.
Camus, Albert .... 92 + refs., 93
Carter, Steve 9, 11
Castro, Fidel 102
Charlton, Bruce .... 24 ref.
Christofides, Dr. Andy .... 10, 11, 178 + ref., 208
Churchill, Winston 109, 110
Clausius, Rudolph 33
Clinton, Hillary 169
Conder, Josiah 85, 192
Copernicus, Nicolaus 130
Cousin, Anne 22

Select Index

Cox, Professor Brian ....50, 51, 53-56, 147 + ref., 151 + ref.
Craig, Professor William Lane.. 79, 175
Cranmer, Archbishop Thomas 204
Crick, Francis H. C.. 157
Cronin, H...155 ref.
Cush 104
Daniel, the Prophet 186, 187
Darwin, Charles & Darwinian 11, 17, 33, 44, 128, 132, 133, 134, 135 + ref.,
.... 136 + ref., 137, 138ref., 139, 154, 155 + ref., 156, 158 + ref., 160, 166
Darwin, Erasmus ....132, 133 + refs., 134
David, King.....107-8, 111, 116, 147, 148, 176, 177, 180, 185, 186, 187, 191
Davies, W. H. 11, 20-21
Domitian, Emperor.. 197
Donnelly, Professor Ted ....76 + ref.
Dowker, Professor Fay...56 + ref.
Dunne, J. W. 24
Edison, Thomas... 38, 109, 110
Edward VI, King 204
Edwards, Jonathan .... 68, 69 + ref.
Eiffel, Gustave 104, 153-154
Einstein, Albert................ 33-36 + ref., 37, 38, 42, 47, 49, 50, 55, 56, 88, 122
Eliot, T.S. .... 78, 113 ref.
Emmel, T. C...163 ref.
Epicurus... 127, 128
Eve 94, 95, 168, 185
Faithfull, Dr. Nigel T. .... 9-10, 15, 18, 80 refs., 95 ref., 208
Faraday, Michael.. 17, 42-46, 49, 109, 110, 206 refs.
Flavel, John.. 64 + ref., 183 + ref.
Fry, Elizabeth.. 171
Gabriel, the Angel 149, 182, 187-188
Galileo Galilei 130
Galton, Sir Francis.. 139, 140
Garnett, William... 47 ref., 57 ref.
Glas, John 43
God 9, 10, 11, 12, 13, 14, 15, 16, 17, 18, 20, 23, 24, 25, 28, 29, 31, 32,
.... 33, 34, 35, 36, 39, 40, 41, 42, 43, 44, 47, 48, 52, 54, 62, 63, 64, 67,
.... 68, 69, 72, 73 + ref., 76, 77, 79 + ref., 80, 81, 82, 83, 84, 85, 93,
.... 94, 95, 96, 97, 98, 99, 100, 101, 102, 103, 104 + ref., 105, 106, 107,

Select Index

.... 108, 110, 111, 113, 114, 115, 116, 119, 121, 124, 125, 126, 129, 131,
.... 134, 135, 136, 137, 144, 148, 149, 150, 151, 159, 160, 161, 163,
.... 167, 168, 169, 170, 171, 173-205, 205 ref.
Grigg, Russell M. .... 135 ref.
Gross, J. B. .... 164 ref.
Harris, Howel 130
Hart, Joseph 205
Hastings, Lady Selina, Countess of Huntingdon 130
Heisenberg, Werner 37-38
Henry, Matthew .... 66 + ref; 95
Henry VIII, King 202
Herod, King 194
Hertz, Heinrich 49
Hitler, Adolf 138
Hupfeld, Herman 36
Hutchinson, Ian .... 206 ref.
Isaiah, the Prophet 149, 185-188
Jeremiah, the Prophet 149
Jesus Christ 10, 11, 14, 15, 17, 42, 63, 65, 77, 79, 81, 85, 94, 101, 102,
.... 108, 111, 116, 117, 135, 142, 145, 149, 150, 168, 169, 177,
.... 179, 180, 181, 182, 183, 185, 186, 187, 188, 190, 191,
.... 192, 193, 194, 195, 196, 197, 198 + ref., 199, 200
Joanna 195
John, the Apostle .... 67, 69, 77, 79, 80, 83, 84 ref., 85, 117, 145, 150, 168,
.... 178, 180, 181, 184, 189, 191-194, 200
Joseph, the Carpenter 149, 181
Josephus, Titus Flavius 195-196
Kennedy, President J. F. 26.102
Khrushchev, Nikita 102
Kidman, Nicole 39-40
Latimer, Bishop Hugh 202-203, 204
Lavoisier, Antoine Laurent 122
Leconte, Jérémy .... 89 ref.
Lloyd-Jones, Dr. D. Martyn .... 74-75 + ref.
Lovejoy, Arthur O. .... 128 ref.
Lucretius 129
Luke, Saint 66, 101, 102, 149, 182, 187, 188, 191, 194, 195, 199
Lyell, Sir Charles 156

~ 211 ~

Select Index

Magdalene, Mary 195
Marcet, Jane 43
Marie-Antoinette, Queen 97
Mark, Saint 81, 111, 169, 187, 204
Marriott, John 127-128
Mary I, Queen 202
Mary, the mother of James 195
Mary, the Virgin 115, 149, 181-182, 187, 188
Mason, John, hymnist 19, 106
Maxwell, James Clerk .... 17, 42, 46, 47 + ref., 48-49, 57, 167, 206 ref.
Mayr, Ernst ....128 ref.
Meyer, Dr. Stephen C. .... 156, 157 + ref., 158-160
Miller, J. Y. ....163 ref.
More, Hannah .... 70 + ref., 80
Morris, Professor Henry .... 104 + ref.
Moses 77, 80, 97, 127, 131, 199
Müller, George 170-171
Napoleon, Emperor 98
Nelson, Horatio 109, 110
Nelson, M. R. ....166 ref.
Newton, Isaac .... 17, 30-32 + ref., 33, 36, 45, 47
Nimrod 104
Noah 83, 99-101, 102, 103, 104
Paley, William 135
Palmer, B. M. ....71 ref.
Parker, J. W. 136
Pascal, Blaise .... 112, 113 + ref., 116
Paul, the Apostle 41, 75, 78, 85, 94, 114, 126, 137, 149, 168,
 .... 177, 178, 179, 180, 181, 182, 192, 195, 197, 199, 201, 205
Pegington, Dr. Chris .... 10, 11, 163 & 165 refs.
Persson, Markus 39
Peter, the Apostle 81, 82, 100, 101, 145, 188, 189, 195, 199, 200
Pilate, Pontius 145, 194, 196, 197
Planck, Max 47, 54
Plato 127, 128, 130, 134
Priestley, J. B. ....24 + refs
Priestley, Joseph .... 25 + ref., 131 + refs., 132, 136
Priscilla 197

Select Index

Ray, Haleigh A. ....163 ref.
Reeves, Professor Michael ....62 + ref., 184 + ref., 194
Ridley, Bishop Nicholas 202
Romme, Charles-Gilbert 98
Rowland, Daniel 130
Rowley, Francis H. 183
Russell, Bertrand 36
Ryle, Bishop J. C. ....83, 84 + refs., 202 ref.
Sandeman, Robert 43
Shaftesbury, Lord 171
Shakespeare, William 27-28
Shapiro, Professor Irwin 55
Solomon, King 28, 29, 112, 113, 116, 183
Spinoza 35
Spurgeon, Charles Haddon 109, 110
Stalin, Joseph ....98, 142-143 + ref. , 146
Stopes, Marie C. C. .... 140-141 + refs.
Suetonius, Gaius Tranquillus .... 197 + ref.
Szreter, Simon R. S. ....140 ref.
Tacitus, Publius Cornelius ....196-197 + ref.
Tallus 197
Thales of Miletus 125
Theophilus 194
Thomas, Brian ....164 ref.
Thomas, Dylan 92
Thomas, Dr. Geoff 10, 11, 12-15, 200
Thornwell, James Henley .... 71 + ref., 80, 81
Tiberius, Claudius Caesar 197
Tillotson, Dr. John ....65 + ref.
Tozer, Aiden Wilson .... 73 + ref., 77
Turok, Professor Neil 53
Tyndale, William 201-202
Tyndall, J. ....206 ref.
Van der Laan, Professor Harry ....58 + ref.
Vaughan, Henry 61
Virgil 20
Waring, Anna Letitia 184
Watson, James 157

Select Index

Watts, Isaac .... 43, 67-68 + ref., 80, 206 ref.
Wedgewood, Josiah 138
Wells, H. G. 23-24, 26, 144
Wesley, Charles 108, 130
Wesley, David J. .... 163 ref.
Wesley, John 130
White, A. J. Monty .... 152 + ref.
Whitefield, George 130
Williams, William 130
Winslow, Octavius .... 180 + refs.
Wood, Todd C. .... 161 ref.
Zechariah 194

www.ingramcontent.com/pod-product-compliance
Lightning Source LLC
Chambersburg PA
CBHW052130010526
44113CB00034B/1445